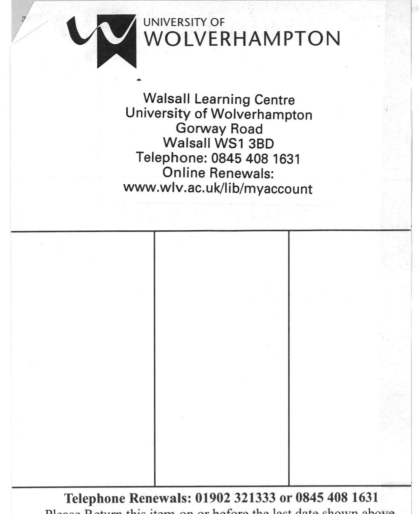

UNIVERSITY OF
WOLVERHAMPTON

Walsall Learning Centre
University of Wolverhampton
Gorway Road
Walsall WS1 3BD
Telephone: 0845 408 1631
Online Renewals:
www.wlv.ac.uk/lib/myaccount

Telephone Renewals: 01902 321333 or 0845 408 1631
Please Return this item on or before the last date shown above.
Fines will be charged if items are returned late.
See tariff of fines displayed at the Counter.

Physical Education Teachers'
Lives and Careers

Physical Education Teachers' Lives and Careers:
PE, Sport and Educational Status

Kathleen M. Armour and
Robyn L. Jones

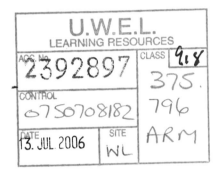

FALMER PRESS
Taylor & Francis Group

UK   Falmer Press, 1 Gunpowder Square, London
USA   Falmer Press, Taylor & Francis Inc., 1900 Frost Road, Suite 101,
          Bristol, PA 19007

First published in 1998

A catalogue record for this book is available from the British Library

Library of Congress Cataloging-in-Publication Data are available on request

ISBN 0 7507 0818 2 cased
ISBN 0 7507 0817 4 paper

Jacket design by Caroline Archer

Typeset in 11/13 Times by
Graphicraft Typesetters Ltd., Hong Kong.

Printed in Great Britain by Biddles Ltd., Guildford and King's Lynn on paper which has a specified pH value on final paper manufacture of not less than 7.5 and is therefore 'acid free'.

Every effort has been made to contact copyright holders for their permission to reprint material in this book. The publishers would be grateful to hear from any copyright holder who is not here acknowledged and will undertake to rectify any errors or omissions in future editions of this book.

Contents

Part One   **Introduction**   1

Chapter 1   Introduction   3
               Purpose and Structure   3
               The Broader Education Context   5
               Writing Stories and Painting Portraits:
                     Data Collection and Interpretation   6
               The Researchers: Authors, Writers, Artists?   10
               The Teacher Respondents   13
               The Theme Chapters   15

Part Two   **The Teachers' Stories**   19

Chapter 2   Jane   23

Chapter 3   Pete   29

Chapter 4   Arnold   36

Chapter 5   Diane   42

Chapter 6   Laura   48

Chapter 7   Edgar   54

Chapter 8   Maggie   62

Chapter 9   Grant   70

Part Three   **The Theme Chapters**   77

Chapter 10   Physical Education and Sport: Conflict
                or Continuum?   79

Chapter 11   Striving for Status in the Education Club:
                'Us', 'Them' and 'We'   93

Chapter 12   Caring in Physical Education: A Three-dimensional
                Analysis   108

Contents

Chapter 13   Moving in, Moving Along and Moving Out:
Career Progression in Physical Education   123

Chapter 14   Physical Education, Sport and Educational Status:
The Case for Fundamental Research   134

References   143

Index   151

Part One

Introduction

Introduction

Purpose and Structure

When we're talking about physical education, we're really talking about education . . . but sport is just doing it. (Jane)

We are teaching sport, but we're using that sport as a vehicle to open up a lot of other avenues. (Maggie)

I've never really known the difference . . . I can't see it because we do a load of sports in physical education. (Grant)

This book explores the complex links between sport, education and physical education, as expressed and experienced by practising physical education teachers. It is based on the assumption that, in creating and fulfilling the simultaneous roles of teacher, coach and sports participant, the physical education teacher can be viewed as the embodiment of the sport/education/ physical education relationship. However, theoretical debates over the years have pointed to tensions in that relationship, suggesting that there is a fundamental conflict between the goals of sport and those of physical education. Furthermore, there is a wealth of evidence pointing to the lowly status accorded to physical education in the education system. Meanwhile, the physical education teacher tries to manage a role where, among other requirements, knowledge and experience of all three aspects — sport, education and physical education — are essential components of the job. It is no wonder that this is, at times, a challenging task.

The broad purpose of this book is to seek to understand more about the ways in which physical education teachers accommodate conflicting role expectations from schools, the physical education profession and the sporting and wider community. More specifically, the focus is upon how teachers establish their personal philosophies and professional practices in physical education, how their personal involvement in sport has influenced that process, and how they manage to create and maintain a rewarding — or at least tolerable — role for themselves in the face of a largely unsupportive education system. In order to achieve such an understanding, the book is based on the stories of eight practising physical education teachers. The teachers, who were at various stages in their careers, participated in a detailed interview process. In the first stage of the process, the interviews centred on teachers' personal philosophies for physical education, their beliefs about success and failure for themselves and for the subject, and their views on support for physical education within the school structure. In the second stage, the emphasis shifted to a focused life-story approach where teachers discussed their personal involvement in sport from early childhood, through their school and higher education experiences and onto their teaching careers. The specific aim was to gain an holistic understanding of the interviewees as physical education teachers.

The book is organized into three main sections. The purpose of this introductory section is to clarify the rationale for the project and to provide some background detail on the research process upon which the book is based. Included in this is an overview of the broad education context in which the teachers' stories are located, an introduction to the teacher respondents, some information on ourselves as the interpreters of the teachers' stories, and a brief description of the four 'theme' chapters which follow the teacher case-studies. Comment on the interview process by some of the teachers concludes the chapter. In Part Two (Chapters 2–9) the data from the interviews with teachers are presented in individual case-story chapters. Each story is unique, and is informative as a case-study in its own right. However, there are also common themes which emerge as the stories are analysed and are compared with each other, and these are presented, in Part Three, in four 'theme' chapters (Chapters 10–13). The purpose of these four chapters is to locate teachers' comments within the existing literature and to raise key questions about, for example, the relationship between physical education and sport, the functions and status of physical education in secondary schools and teachers' careers in physical education. This strategy, of presenting the teachers' stories both individually and in the form of emerging themes can, we believe, offer considerable depth to our understanding of key issues in the lives and careers of physical education teachers. It also offers the reader two ways of reading the book. Each chapter has been written to be complete in itself, therefore it is possible to begin with either the theme chapters or the teachers' stories.

A final point to be made is that although the teachers are all from England, it became apparent, by reference to international research, that their experiences are mirrored across the world (see, particularly, Chapter 11). In some ways this is quite remarkable, given the historical variations in the development of both physical education and sport, and the differences in the education systems which pertain. At the same time, and retaining a due sense of caution about the scope of this research, it does lend some support to the life-story approach which has been adopted and provides a justification for our pleas, made in the conclusion, for fundamental, international research in physical education.

The Broader Education Context

The interviews with teachers were conducted between 1989 and 1996. All of the teachers had been educated and trained in England, and all were teaching in English schools at the time of the interviews. In order to provide a context for their stories, and to clarify some of their comments for international readers, the purpose of this section is to present a brief overview of the education system during that period.

The earliest interviews were those conducted at Citylimits High School in 1989 (Chapters 2–5). In 1988, a major change in education was signaled by the Conservative Government with the introduction of the Education Reform Act (ERA). This act established, for the first time, a National Curriculum in all state schools in England and Wales. Physical education was identified as a National Curriculum subject, with the first official documentation being produced in 1992 (DES/WO, 1992). This document specified programmes of study for pupils in physical education at each 'Key Stage' (KS) of their education: KS 1 denotes pupils up to the age of 7; KS 2 includes pupils from 7–11; KS 3 from 11–14; and KS 4 from 14–16 (DES, 1989). It also specified targets against which pupils' progress could be measured. However, the requirements for many subjects, including physical education, were simplified in 1995. In particular, the assessment burden was reduced (DFE/WO, 1995). Two other features of the ERA are also relevant. Local Management of Schools (LMS) established a formula for allocating funds to a school based on the number of pupils it could attract. In a related initiative, schools were also offered the opportunity to apply for Grant Maintained Status (GMS). This allows schools to be more autonomous as they receive a direct grant from central government, instead of receiving an allocation via the local education authority. Such schools are commonly known as 'opted out' (of local authority) schools. Citylimits High School applied for, and was granted GMS, shortly after our interviews. Underpinning the whole structure is the regular and rigorous inspection of schools by the semi-independent Office for Standards in Education (OFSTED). Schools are expected to demonstrate that they are delivering the National Curriculum, and inspection reports are made available to the general public.

Several teachers' stories make reference to the public examination system and to GCSE examinations. All pupils take a common examination, in a range of subjects, at the age of 16. This is known as the General Certificate of Secondary Education (GCSE). At the age of 18, pupils take Advanced Level ('A' Level) examinations in a reduced range of subjects. In recent years, examination courses in physical education have become ever more popular, with courses in 'Physical Education' and 'Sports Studies' running parallel to each other. As a broad generalization, there has tended to be more scope for practical work in those entitled 'Physical Education', although the differences are often minimal. Examination preparation has become an established feature of the work of many physical education teachers. Finally, the current climate in physical education is influenced by another political factor. The previous Prime Minister, John Major, professed a personal interest in sport in schools. He initiated a policy statement entitled 'Sport, Raising the Game' (DNH, 1995) which placed emphasis upon the role of competitive team sports within physical education. Although this was broadly welcomed, particularly where it seemed to hint at increased resources for schools, some caution was expressed by many in the physical education profession who envisage a broader focus for physical education (Penney and Evans, 1997).

Writing Stories and Painting Portraits: Data Collection and Interpretation

Wright Mills (1959) suggests that:

> Order as well as disorder is relative to viewpoint: to come to an orderly understanding of men (sic) and societies requires a set of viewpoints that are simple enough to make understanding possible, yet comprehensive enough to permit us to include in our views the range and depth of human variety. The struggle for such viewpoints is the first and continuing struggle of social science. (p. 133)

The belief that social science is about 'human variety' is a guiding principle for this work. Competing ideologies on sport, education and physical education are understood as the result of a complex amalgam of teachers' personal life experiences and their interaction with the broader social structures of departments and schools. The complexity of these processes is daunting, and Wright Mills (1959) identifies the need for a 'sociological imagination' in order to 'grasp history and biography and the relations between the two in society' (p. 6). Evans and Davies (1988) further point out that 'the interplay of self, biography and social structure lies at the heart of the sociological enterprise' (p. 10). Hence, the teachers in this account are located primarily within the context of their own life-stories, but also in the immediate structure of a physical education department, a specific school and, of course, within the broader structure of the education system in England. These structural layers are particularly evident in the first four teacher stories, because all the teachers work in the same physical education department. Even within that same structure, however, the difference between the teachers' stories, the 'human variety', is clearly in evidence. So, for the reader, some stories will resonate with personal experience and some will clearly conflict. This is, perhaps, both the strength and the weakness of the approach taken in this book. Terkel (1981) clarifies it thus:

> Each of the subjects is, I feel, uniquely himself. Whether he is an arche-typal American figure, reflecting thought and condition over and beyond himself, is for the reader to judge, calling upon his own experience, obser-vations, and an occasional look in the mirror. (cited in Lawn and Barton, 1981, p. 245)

No attempt therefore is made by us, the authors, to generalize from these eight teachers' stories to *all* 'physical education teachers'. Rather, we have sought to write interesting stories which paint colourful and accurate por-traits of the teacher respondents. Our aim is to ensure that the reader can *understand* these teachers and their philosophies: a task Wolcott (1990) describes as 'a more ambitious activity' than 'merely knowing' (p. 146). Thus, we hope that readers will generalize into the context of their own lives and careers — 'an occasional look in the mirror' (Lawn and Barton, 1981, p. 245) — and the lives and careers of colleagues. If the result is a greater understanding between very different individuals within physical education departments, then the book has fulfilled a useful purpose. Furthermore, in highlighting and analysing four themes which arise in very different ways in the teachers' stories, it is hoped that, here again, greater understanding of some of these issues will result. For as Woods (1990) points out: 'recogni-tion can lead to possibilities' (p. 144).

The Research Interviews

As befits the nature of the project, the interviews were 'reflexive' in nature (Hammersley and Atkinson, 1983), in that specific questions were not pre-pared beforehand, although provisional themes for framing questions had been developed (Sparkes and Templin, 1992). An invitation was, therefore, extended to the teachers to explore a range of issues in collaboration with the interviewer (Powney and Watts, 1987). In this way, as was noted earlier, we hoped to construct a portrait of each respondent, particularly in terms of their current philosophies of physical education and the life-journeys they had taken to arrive at those beliefs. The concept of reflexivity was central to the undertaking, as we aimed to discover how the respondents understood *their* world. This reflected the need to explore the subjective reality of the individual, placing the personal physical education experience within that of the wider contextual existence. The insider's perspective was, therefore, at the heart of the research, with the respondents' meanings and interpretations of people and events being significant. Indeed, such information 'is of great importance in any attempt to explain why people act in certain ways rather than others' (Sparkes and Templin, 1992, p. 121). To this end, Geertz' (1973) concept of 'thick description' was helpful, which 'does not relate to complexities objectively described (but) to the particular perceptions of the actors' (Stake, 1995, p. 42). The goal of understanding, as opposed to describing, the lives and careers of these teachers was, therefore, central.

With this in mind, although the interviews were taped to ensure that a complete and accurate record of the data was obtained, notes were also taken on the context in which assertions were made and of any innuendoes implied. Indeed, it is these contextual subtleties of behaviour and expression that can be vital keys to understanding (Locke, 1989). After the interviews, transcripts were offered to the respondents for checking. In the case of the last four interviews, the final stories were also discussed with the teachers. We believe that this was a particularly valuable exercise, given that 'agreements and disagreements are illuminating in themselves' (Sparkes, 1992, p. 32). Indeed, such discussions further enhanced and refined our interpretations, making the consultations not so much 'a test of the "truth", but an opportunity for reflexive elaboration' (Sparkes, 1992, p. 33). We were thus, very much aware of the need to be accurate in terms of the meaning expressed from the respondents' perspective during the interviews, as 'accuracy is a criterion relative to the purposes for which it is sought' (Runciman, 1983, p. 97). At the same time, in adopting an interpretive perspective, we were also conscious of the possibility of the existence of many 'truths', realities and interpretations. Therefore, we had to use our judgment, as interpreters, in the final presentation of the data from interviews.

But, is this research valid? Well — are the teachers' lives and careers valid? The question appears to make little sense in that context. Even so, a consideration of validity is central to any research-based work and, to this end, we found Maxwell's (1992) guidelines to be helpful. His initial categories of 'descriptive' and 'interpretive' validity correspond to our attempts, not only to record the data accurately, but also to establish the intended meaning. In relation to Maxwell's third category of 'theoretical' validity, an attempt was made to examine the suppositions and constructions arising from the data and to locate these within the existing body of knowledge in physical education — the four theme chapters in the final section of the book. In contrast to considerations of descriptive and interpretive validity therefore, the drive for theoretical validity focused on the explanatory potential of the data, rather than their factual or interpretive accuracy. In the final event, however, and in further support of Wolcott (1990), we endorse Maxwell's conclusion that 'understanding is a more fundamental concept for qualitative research than validity' (1992, p. 281). The key lies therefore, 'not with the validity or invalidity of the data, but rather with the inferences drawn from them' (Hammersley and Atkinson, 1983, p. 191). Thus, it is, that the various phases of the research process merge: the stories teachers tell initially, the portraits we, as researchers, then paint from those stories and, in four of the cases, the teachers' reactions to our efforts.

Qualitative studies of this nature do not usually claim generalizability in the traditional research sense. However, even though meaning can be apparent in a single instance or event, our analysis of the interview data was based on the premise that 'the search for meaning is often a search for patterns (and) for consistency' (Stake, 1995, p. 78). Therefore, where generalizations can be made, 'they usually take place through the development of a theory that not only makes sense of the particular persons studied, but also shows how the same process in different situations can lead to different results' (Becker, 1990, p. 240). Certainly, the notion of 'difference' is evident in this research and it reinforces the earlier explanation offered by Terkel (in Lawn and Barton, 1981).

To summarize, in focusing upon the constraints and possibilities of both individual action and broader structures in education, the research interviews recognized both 'subjective and objective dimensions to a career in teaching' (Sparkes and Templin, 1992, p. 121) in the drive to understand more about physical education teachers and their philosophies.

The Interview Framework

In-depth interviews were conducted with eight secondary school physical education teachers of various ages and levels of experience. Each respondent was interviewed twice, with each interview lasting approximately two hours. The main purpose of the first interview was to obtain detailed data on the individual's personal beliefs about the nature and purpose of physical education. This session was thus, *physical education centred* focusing on the following broad areas:

1   the individual's personal view of the role of physical education in a secondary school;
2   what makes for a 'successful' physical education department, subject and teacher;

3 the difference between physical education and sport;

4 possible conflict between one's own philosophy regarding the subject and those held by departmental colleagues; and,

5 knowledge of the perceptions of related others (e.g. senior managers, teachers, parents, pupils and governors) about the subject.

The principal purpose of the second interview was to obtain detailed information on the teachers' life-stories. Although some general contextual information was sought, the objective was to explore the respondents' experiences in sport, physical activity and physical education. The focus here was thus very much person (self) centred, with the general areas for investigation relating to differing life phases. More specifically, these included:

1 early family influences;

2 experiences of sport and physical education at primary and secondary school;

3 details of higher education; and,

4 current career issues and speculation on the future from a personal and professional viewpoint.

The data are presented, in the teachers' stories, in the order corresponding to the order of the interview.

The Researchers: Authors, Writers, Artists?

Who are we — Armour and Jones? Kathy and Robyn? We, too, have many identities and roles. Acutely aware that interpretive theory and data are convincing only in so far as the reader allows, we considered it appropriate to provide more information about ourselves than is usual. In undertaking this joint project, we learnt much about both the teacher respondents and the issues analysed in the later chapters. But what of ourselves? Certainly we felt the reader was entitled to an outline of our position in relation to the research process and the respondents, as well as information regarding our respective backgrounds in physical education and sport. Far from seeking to produce an 'author evacuated text' (Geertz, 1988), we saw ourselves (and our interpretations) as being integral to the work and, therefore, omnipresent in the text — so the inclusion of a self-portrait seemed inescapable. But oh, how difficult to do! How much easier to be anonymous, superior, distanced, objective! We did find that this relatively small task highlighted the various skills which we needed in order to produce this book: researchers — first and foremost, based on the requirements of our jobs and our doctorate experiences; authors — in terms of conceiving of the project, undertaking it and organizing it into a particular format; writers — a technical skill required to write the initial sections of the book and the theme chapters in the final section; and finally artists — the task of painting portraits of the individual teachers and of making them interesting, colourful and absorbing. In writing about ourselves, all of those roles were crystallized, reinforcing Wolcotts's (1990) assertion that 'Qualitative researchers need to be storytellers' (p. 17) and extending it even further.

We also learnt an interesting point about each other. We approached this joint project from opposite ends of the sport/physical education spectrum: as a physical education teacher (Armour) and as a very successful sportsperson (Jones). We simply hadn't realized this until the end of the project, but it certainly provides yet more support for the consideration of this book as 'spoken and written from many sites' (Sparkes, 1995, p. 160).

Kathleen Armour

I am a 39-year-old academic, wife and mother. I think I'll be 39 for ever. I caught my passion for physical education from an enthusiastic and committed physical education teacher. Although I was an able sports girl, I was not exceptional and I entered higher education for the express purpose of learning how to teach. None of my degree experience, including teaching practice, provided me with a role model as effective as my own secondary school physical education teacher.

Having taught physical education in a secondary school for four years, I became restless. With no particular aim in mind, I registered for a Master's degree in education and, for the next two years, combined full-time work with part-time study. Then, fate stepped in and I was offered some part-time teaching, and then a full-time post, in higher education. And there I have remained to date, gathering a PhD and three children along the way.

Like other teachers in this book, I recognize that involvement in sport at school contributed to my personal development. I was never close to the pinnacles of excellence, and perhaps that is why I have only really experienced the good things that sport can offer. It may also explain my own personal difficulty in seeing sport and physical education as separate entities — I experienced them as one and taught them as one. However, the teachers in this book are all different — to me and from each other. It would take a brave person to generalize, with any confidence, about 'physical education teachers'. Rather, this book is about how some teachers understand and explain themselves and their own philosophies. It is also borne of my fascination with people — I enjoy interviewing them. It is always challenging and stimulating: I always learn. This is not to assume that respondents feel the same, as some of them make clear in their comments about the interview process. But I do have considerable experience as a research interviewer, and this seems to result in a better process for the respondents.

Now I'm a parent. I hope my children will have an interest, even a passion, for sport and many forms of physical activity, but not an obsession. I hope they will encounter knowledgable and caring teachers and coaches who will teach them skills so they can access activities. I trust that those teachers will contribute to their personal and social development — but I don't look specifically to physical education teachers for that — rather I see it as a general function of education and, primarily, of me as a parent. And I hope that none of my children shows exceptional talent in any one sport. If they do, I hope no-one sees it.

Robyn Jones

My research background originates in the sociology of sport; chipping away at the monolithic topics of race and gender. This reflects a fundamental interest in social equity and minority issues, an engagement born of experience. More recently, I have developed research projects using systematic observation instruments in both the teaching and coaching environments. This has led to a desire to undertake more qualitative investigation into the world of the sporting practitioner, in order to further explore and understand the pressures and conflicts facing physical education teachers and coaches.

After being released from a professional football club at 18, I entered Swansea University in 1979 and successfully completed a bachelors degree in the social sciences. In 1984 I graduated from Bangor University with an MA degree in Comparative Physical Education. Believing my focus to be sport, as distinct from physical education, I rejected an opportunity to do a PGCE. Instead, I began working in a variety of administrative posts in both local and central government, initially in my native North Wales and later in London. Finally, in 1989, I realized a long held ambition and entered the doctoral programme in Health and Human Sciences at the University of Southern Mississippi in the US. Following the completion of my PhD, I returned to London in 1992, resurrected my semi-professional football career, married, and acquired two children and a mortgage in quick succession! I began working in higher education a year later and am now a senior lecturer in a Department of Sport Sciences. My principal teaching responsibilities are in sport sociology and research methods.

A common thread in how my life has unfolded to date has been sport, and particularly football. It has provided significant input to the construction of my identity, in addition to supplying some of the most emotional moments of my life. I am presently involved in coaching, and although continuing to play veterans' football, I still mourn the loss of the feeling that only quality performances against high class opposition can ever give. I often ponder on how sport will influence the lives of my daughters, if at all. If either has the talent and desire to carve out a career as a professional athlete, I'll certainly not let the stifling rationale of 'get an education first' stand in the way. I see no reason why both cannot be pursued simultaneously, but if one does have to take a back seat for a while, our growing ranks of mature students are living evidence that university is open at any time.

The Teacher Respondents

The eight teachers presented in this book are from four different physical education departments. The first four stories (Jane, Pete, Arnold and Diane) are about teachers from one department in a school called Citylimits High school. In this instance, the differences between the stories of individuals who all work, ostensibly, in one common structure, is a notable feature. Following these are stories about two teachers (Laura and Edgar) who work together in a school known as Enterprise High School. Their stories highlight the strength of common and conflicting philosophies on physical education, and the legacy of personal life-experiences. The last two stories are about unconnected teachers in two further schools. Maggie is teaching in a comprehensive school and Grant in a grammar school.

The interviews at Citylimits High School took place in the late 1980s, in the context of a wider ethnographic study into the 'life' of a physical education department. Although the National Curriculum was being mooted at the time, the department at Citylimits saw little merit in panic and had decided they would make any required changes very slowly. Hence, it hardly features in their comments. It is interesting to reflect on other changes which have occurred since then which do, or do not, change our reading of those stories. The interviews with the other four teachers took place during 1996. Here again, with the National Curriculum fully in place, it is interesting to note that the teachers volunteered little comment about it in the interviews, although in reading their final case-study stories, they all thought that perhaps they should have made more of it. Both Grant and Maggie added some extra comments on the National Curriculum to their stories. If, perhaps, we had interviewed in the early 1990s, we may have encountered more debate about implementation. Interestingly, in comparing the earlier and the more recent interviews, there is little to indicate that there was any time lapse. This may be an indication of the durability of the core activities of being a physical education teacher, a point raised by Laura, one of the respondents.

In all the case-study chapters, extensive quotes from the teachers are included. These are accurate in meaning, although somewhat sanitized in style. None of the teachers felt that readers would have much interest in the numerous 'you knows' and 'uhms' which pepper normal speech. As one teacher said of his many 'you knows': 'to say it in the run of conversation is one thing, but to make people read it again and again would be pointless'. We agreed.

On Being Interviewed

In addition to their comments about the completed case-study stories, we also asked the four recently interviewed teachers to note down any feelings they had about being involved in the whole research process. Did they, for example, enjoy being interviewed? Was it embarrassing or enjoyable? How did they feel afterwards? Three teachers chose to comment:

> In terms of the interviewing process, I was unsure as to the focus of the discussion. Most of my comments were 'off the cuff' and one aspect of my philosophies seemed to come through more sub-consciously than I'd realized.

> The interview provided an opportunity to reflect and contemplate aspects of the occupation that one rarely takes time to consider. Since then, I have found myself to be more reflective about day-to-day occurences. If I was to be interviewed now, I might emphasize some other aspects of my philosophies. (Laura)

> . . . after both interviews had finished, I felt there were one or two things I would have liked to have said/not said . . . the interviews were not uncomfortable, but they were illuminating and embarrassing. The process of having my life/career scrutinized did make me feel apprehensive after the interviews and when you said you were sending this case-study I was rather worried as to how I would come across and how my philosophy for P.E. would seem. The picture you have of yourself is not always the same as others have of you!' (Grant)

> The interviews were great to be a part of. It was nice to have someone to talk to about something very important to me. Never mind the kids calling each other 'boffins', there is a great deal of cynicism among teachers and it isn't always fashionable to actually be enthusiastic about your subject area, or the kids, in front of other staff. Professional dialogue is often dominated by disciplinary issues rather than curriculum development.

I did feel honoured to be taking part in the book. It's important to everyone to feel that your opinion might be worth something. However, I can't
guarantee that future readers won't fall asleep during [some] sections, I'm
sure they might be more stimulated by stories of debauchery in the college
bar! (Maggie)

These three teachers also provided some written feedback about their feelings as they read their completed case-study stories. These are included at
the end of the appropriate chapters.

The Theme Chapters

The final section of the book is divided into four chapters (Chapters 10–13).
Each chapter focuses upon a theme which was identified by both authors
as being significant when the teachers' stories were considered together. Of
course there are others — the discussion could have developed in so many
different areas. However, we hope that these chapters will add to our knowledge of some well-worn issues by locating the teachers' stories in the body
of existing literature, whilst also identifying new areas for debate and research.

In Chapter 10, the relationship between physical education and sport
is examined in some depth. This relationship has long been of interest to
academics in both fields in Britain as elsewhere. Historically, the two areas
shared similar ideals. Practitioners in both the worlds of sport and education tended to view physical education, primarily, as a training ground for
young sporting talent. More recently, and particularly in the late 1970s and
the 1980s, physical educationists stressed the broad educational aims of their
work. They preferred to distance themselves from the influence of the sporting community which was perceived as placing undue emphasis on elite
sport at the expense of mass participation: as Talbot (1987) commented,
'the game is not the thing, the child is'. Thus, some conflict between the
two perspectives was inevitable, and academic debate in physical education
reflected that tension.

More recently in Britain, there are signs that the worlds of physical
education and sport are converging once again, but with a new understanding of the appropriate roles for each party. A number of agencies are building upon what are perceived as 'natural' links: for example, the National
Coaching Foundation draws upon the personal sporting interests of physical
education teachers in 'Champion Coaching'; some governing bodies of sport
have developed curriculum materials to coincide with the interest generated
by major sporting events; and the Government, in the policy statement 'Sport:
Raising the Game' stressed the imperative for partnership:

> Promoting sport in schools and beyond does of course depend on partner-
> ship between schools, further and higher education institutions, sporting
> bodies, local authorities, clubs, the private sector and Government. No
> single partner can act alone; each partner must pull its own weight and
> maintain a clear view of the importance of sport within society and of the
> importance of achieving the broadest possible access to sporting oppor-
> tunity. (Dept. National Heritage, 1995, p. 40)

The Physical Education Association of the UK has made a generally positive
response to this government initiative. Almond, Harrison and Laws (1996),
state:

> The Physical Education Association is extremely pleased with the public
> statements made by both the Prime Minister and the Government which
> help to raise the profile of physical education and sport. (p. 7)

Although cautious in some respects, it is interesting to note that Almond
et al. (1996) describe physical education as 'the base of sporting excellence'
(p. 10) and they conclude that 'a spirit of partnership' (p. 11) is essential to
the process of increasing sports participation levels and raising the standard
of sports performances. Clearly, then, the potential exists for a more harmo-
nious relationship between physical education and sport, although others
in the profession are less certain of the benefits of such links (Penney and
Evans, 1997). It is interesting to remember, however, that amid all these
variations in philosophy, the physical education teacher continues to rep-
resent the embodiment of both sporting and educational perspectives — as
both teacher and coach, or teacher and sports performer, for example. In
examining this issue, therefore, the intention is to place the reality of that
embodiment at the forefront. In particular, by placing physical education
teachers at the centre of the analysis, rather than schools, sport, or pupils, it
becomes increasingly difficult to identify any logical distance between physical education and sport. Rather, what emerges, is the way in which low
status in an educational context impacts upon both activities.

Chapter 11 furthers the investigation into low status by examining the
place of physical education and sport in the wider context of the secondary
school. This raises important, ongoing status issues which face physical education teachers. Bell (1986) notes that physical education departments 'are an
interesting example of the interrelationship between a subject or discipline
. . . and the school structure' (p. 99), and he identifies the practical nature
of physical education as a central status problem for physical educationists.
Similarly, in the teachers' case-study stories, the tension between low-status,
practical subjects and high-status, 'academic' subjects is a recurrent feature.

This is, perhaps, unsurprising as numerous studies, both national and international, confirm that status concerns for physical education teachers are an enduring reality (Moreira, Sparkes and Fox, 1995; Stroot, Collier, O'Sullivan and England, 1994; Sparkes, Templin and Schempp, 1990). In this respect, it would appear that physical education has yet to counter charges made by educational philosophers that it is not a serious subject (Peters, 1966) and, in a classic snub, that claims for its educational worth are 'disreputable' (White, 1973). There are numerous reasons for the endurance of these status issues, some of which can be traced to the physical education profession itself, and some of which seem to be the responsibility of the broader education community. Brooker and Macdonald (1995) contend that: 'Historically, PE has been slow to define its place in the school curriculum' (p. 108). In an analysis of Australian education they note that physical education has been viewed, variously, as health education, sport education, science and academic study. Similarly, in this country, there are a number of discourses operating within the broad framework of physical education. The teachers in this book identified health education and academic study as knowledge claims which could enhance their status. However, these 'status solutions' appear to have made little impact upon the educational status of physical education and sport, reinforcing Bell's (1986) earlier point that it is the practical nature of physical education which causes the status problems.

Chapter 12 investigates teachers' claims that physical education has a unique role in the social and moral education of pupils. This appears to be another example of a 'status solution' and the claim would appear to have three separate dimensions: the 'caring' teacher of physical education; social/moral values inherent in the subject matter; and opportunities for social/moral education afforded by the open learning environment in physical education. Noddings' (1984) analysis of 'caring' in education is adopted as a framework for discussion in the three dimensions, and comparisons are drawn with the work of Rovegno and Kirk (1995). Although it is difficult to substantiate teachers' claims to be educating pupils in the social/moral dimension, it is equally clear that the teachers in this book believed in this as a valued part of their work. However, in investigating the issue in more depth, it becomes clear that such claims may need research evidence to support them. Moreover, as a 'status solution', the social/moral knowledge claim for physical education appears to have failed, dismally.

In Chapter 13, the status problems for physical education converge into what, perhaps, is the only logical outcome: poor career prospects for its teachers. The careers of the case-study teachers are examined in stages. Firstly, 'moving in' to physical education investigates family and school influences upon decisions to enter the profession, the impact of teacher education, and the role of sport in the development of personal philosophies on education and physical education. In the second section, 'moving along', issues which arise in the progress of the teachers' careers are examined and the variable nature of job commitment is considered. Finally, in 'moving out', opportunities for promotion are analyzed and a seemingly inescapable career paradox for the case-study teachers is identified: in justifying physical education in theoretical/esoteric terms, (particularly in the social/moral dimension), and then moving away from the subject base of physical education for promotion, teachers simply reinforce the low status of themselves and their subject. On the other hand, if they stay in the practical context of teaching physical education, their career opportunities are severely limited. The question remains: how can physical education teachers break the cycle of low status?

Chapter 14, the conclusion, attempts to answer that question, by drawing together the threads of the discussion. Five threads are highlighted: the complexity of the status issue, the need for physical education to build on the knowledge of its predecessors, the requirement for 'fundamental research' in physical education, the role of sport in physical education and, lastly, but centrally, the teachers and the imperative to enable them to have confidence in themselves and their subject in an educational setting.

Finally, an earlier comment by Wright Mills (1959) referred to the sociological quest for 'viewpoints that are simple enough to make understanding possible' (p. 133). The decision to base this analysis upon the life-stories of physical education teachers represents an attempt to ground a complex theoretical debate in a real-life context, and thus to aid understanding. The real-life contexts are not, in themselves, simple. However, presentation of key issues through this medium can, we believe, make understanding more likely — and the route more enjoyable.

Part Two

The Teachers' Stories

Citylimits High School

The teacher's voice must speak from an embeddedness within the culture of the particular school, the school system and society in which the teacher lives and works. (Elbaz, 1991, p. 13)

Citylimits High School is located on the outskirts of a large city in the middle of England. It was built in the early 1960s and is fairly typical of its genre — rather plain in design, much glass, overpoweringly hot in the summer and difficult to heat in the winter. Originally, Citylimits High was a secondary modern school. It became fully comprehensive in the early 1980s and, although it has yet to equal the reputation of the former grammar schools in the area, it is highly regarded, over-subscribed, and is generally considered to be 'on the up'. At the time of the interviews, the head strenuously denied rumours that Citylimits was considering 'opting out' of local authority control. Within a year, however, it had done so.

The school's mission, as detailed in its handbook, is to enable all members of the school 'fully to realize their potential'. More specifically, the school sets out to provide a curriculum which 'serves the needs of all pupils as well as of society', and to encourage in pupils both 'a sense of responsibility' and the ability to 'exercise self-discipline'. Ultimately, pupils are to be prepared to 'take their place in the modern adult world': in short, a fairly conservative set of aspirations.

Citylimits High School embraces a number of 'whole school policies' and prides itself on promoting a philosophy of common purpose and joint resolve between pupils, parents and staff. On the whole, staff like the school and feel that they are quite fortunate in their pupils and their facilities. For physical education, the school has reasonable facilities including a dual-use sports hall, extensive playing fields and hardcourt areas — most of which are in a poor state of repair. The physical education department is respected in the locality for its success in local sports competitions and it has a sound reputation within the school — marred somewhat by divisions between the head of department and one member of staff.

The four physical education teachers whose stories are presented in Chapters 2–5 are:

Jane: formerly head of girls' physical education and now head of the combined department. She has taught at Citylimits for six years.

Pete: has taught at Citylimits for 10 years. He also applied for the post of head of the combined department and now resents Jane's appointment. Pete is viewed as 'the odd man out' in the department.

Arnold: formerly the head of boys' physical education but, instead of applying for the head of the combined department, he moved into a role with responsibility for careers and pastoral issues. He has taught at Citylimits for 12 years.

Diane: the youngest member of the department in her second year of teaching.

Chapter 2

Jane

Jane is 42 years old and is the head of department at Citylimits High School. Although she largely enjoys her job, particularly the day-to-day teaching, she gives the impression of being weary. This is due, in part, to the constant battles she feels she must fight for the status of physical education within the school community. In addition, she faces both personal and philosophical opposition within the physical education department, particularly from one male member of staff, Pete. The strain is evident.

Jane followed a traditional route from secondary school into higher education and then straight into teaching. She has since taught in three schools and has been head of department in two. At Citylimits, she is head of a combined department which evolved from separate boys' and girls' sections. Pete also applied for the head of the new department and Jane's success still rankles. Undoubtedly, this is the source of much of the antagonism within the department. At the time of our interviews, Jane had held her position for six years and she was experiencing both professional and personal difficulties.

Jane's philosophy of physical education is shaped by a strong desire to educate pupils for life after secondary school. She describes physical education as: 'a joint thing between good teams . . . and what they actually do in games lessons'. She places great importance on teams, practices and clubs that take place regularly, thus helping pupils to build upon their curriculum interests. In this way she hopes 'pupils will see that they have really got fitness for life'. As she points out:

> I think it's important to get it *in* school right and then get it out of school. And I really see it as a 50:50 thing, and I know there's a lot of people think that it's more important just educating them in school and not worrying too much about out of school, but I think you've got to try and get somewhere between the two.

Throughout the interviews, Jane made it clear that she felt that her view of physical education was under threat and that it was a constant battle to maintain the credibility of the subject within the school. Primarily, she loves

teaching practical activities, yet she was fully supportive of the recent introduction of the GCSE because:

> . . . now we're going onto different committees, and I'm on the academic
> committee which, in the past, you didn't used to count quite as much on
> that. Now they've got to accommodate us for written examinations —
> they've got to see us not only as sport, but as an education.

The notion of sport, as distinct from education, was reinforced in later comments. Jane attempted to make a distinction as follows:

> Well there's a link between the two, but, I think when we're talking about
> physical education we're really talking about education — acquisition of
> knowledge, understanding and . . . give them the feel behind something
> and not *necessarily* that they can do it but at least that they know about
> their bodies and they've got a clear understanding of how to get fit even if
> they're not. But sport is just *doing* it.

Although enjoying teaching practical activities, Jane places increasing value
on theoretical knowledge. She believes that, in an educational context, it
may be more important to learn *about* something than to display the ability
to *do* it. Thus, sport is assigned a non-educational status because it is 'just
doing it'. Furthermore, she sees health education as important — but, here
again, she stresses the value of 'know that'. Her supporting theory of knowledge is further exemplified by her enthusiasm for the GCSE and the importance she attaches to the theoretical elements of the syllabus. For example, she
was delighted to learn from some of her pupils that 'the message is getting
around' about the amount and the difficulty of the theoretical element of the
GCSE in physical education.

The problem Jane faces is that she is fully convinced of the value of
physical education, yet she is increasingly wedded to a view of education
which trivializes much of what she does on a day-to-day basis with the
pupils — the practical activity. Her response to a perceived lack of status
for physical education is to stress the value of the theoretical elements
of the subject. She feels that it is somehow not good enough, in an educational context, to be teaching 'just sport', yet her theoretical emphasis
may be counterproductive. Certainly, the internal tension in Jane's position
causes her some discomfort, perhaps all the more so because sport has been
anything but 'just doing it' in her own life. Furthermore, she would appear
to be reinforcing a rigid dualistic view of pupils by endorsing the super-
iority of the 'ghost' over the 'machine' (Ryle, 1949). The tension might
be alleviated if Jane could draw upon a less rigid form of dualism, or even

a monist philosophy, to square her instincts about 'doing' with her prag-matic approach to gaining respect for physical education in an educational framework.

In Jane's personal life, involvement in sport has been a major feature, from childhood to the present. She is an only child and both parents were interested in and fully supportive of her sporting endeavours. Her parents were teachers and it would appear that they used sport to persuade Jane to consider teaching as a career:

> I said all the time that I was *not* going to teach and the only way to persuade me to go to college was to say 'if all you want to do is to play sport, yes, well just go and play sport for three years and then we can decide what you want to do' and maybe because he [father] could see, I mean he was in a secondary school and he could see that I hadn't (laughs) got ability in a lot of other things, he just let me follow what I *could* do and then sort it out.

Reinforced by her parents' views, Jane still has very little faith in her academic ability and, in that respect, she might be described as a perfect candidate for teaching and for the BEd degree (Woods, 1980; Mardle and Walker, 1980). However, Jane describes her upbringing as 'relaxed', 'happy, not traumatic in any way'. Even adolescence was described as 'no problem, not too traumatic at all' and she speculated that this may explain why she finds conflict in the department (and in her personal life) so difficult to manage. She tends to prefer to 'walk away' as it is 'just too much hassle'.

Jane places a high value upon establishing and maintaining a large circle of friends. Sport has provided ideal opportunities to achieve this and she commented on her social life at each stage in her story. For example, in recalling her secondary education, she describes her academic career as 'fairly average (laughs) didn't do a great deal, just did as little as I could'. However, she managed to achieve the grades she knew were needed for physical education teacher training because 'that's just the sort of person I am'. She thoroughly enjoyed school because 'we had nice mixed groups and we got on well right from the first year'. It was in sport that Jane really excelled and she became closely involved with the physical education depart-ment. Her choice of teacher training establishment was heavily influenced by her teachers:

> ... there was a tradition in the school that all PE teachers came from X college and every year there would be, about, six or seven pupils that went to X. So when I got there, there were loads of people from two or three years above.

Jane placed great emphasis upon her friendship with the physical education teachers and she expressed some regret that she had been unable to develop the same depth of relationship with many of her own pupils.

Jane went to teacher training college in the late 1970s and she describes her experience in enthusiastic terms:

> And on to college! (laughs). *Best three years of my life. Absolutely superb!* I loved it. I had a terrific group of friends — I don't know *how* we got together but after about three months we'd established a group of ten that were in different lecture groups . . . and so in the second year we had to live out and have 'living in rooms', so we had ten people in our room and we've kept in touch really ever since. It was excellent. Everybody was from different areas, different walks of life . . . and we all just got on so well. Socially it was an absolute laugh, and we worked hard as well. We all enjoyed our sport. In fact doing the practical lectures and doing the sport took up most of the time.

Participation in sport and in practical lectures was central for Jane — the theoretical work was something to be 'slugged through'. Certainly she makes it clear that nothing since training has been quite so enjoyable or memorable.

After training Jane had little difficulty finding teaching posts. As she put it: 'all the jobs came so easily'. In her first post she enjoyed extensive facilities and well motivated pupils. However, Jane then married the head of physical education and felt that it was better not to work in the same school as her husband. Her second post was very different: 'small and *very, very* multicultural. Hardly any white children.' Jane thoroughly enjoyed this job. She became head of department and developed lasting relationships with many of the pupils. However, Jane's first marriage ended and, in starting a new relationship, Jane decided that she should move jobs again — this time to be near her new partner. It proved to be more difficult to change jobs at head of department level but, finally, she obtained the post of head of girls' physical education at Citylimits High school. As was noted earlier, this has since changed to encompass both boys' and girls' physical education.

In general, Jane describes her six years at Citylimits as enjoyable and positive, with increasing reservations recently. Early in post she was involved with physical education examination courses and recently she has embraced the GCSE. In both cases, the examination was viewed as a route to academic respectability. Currently, as was noted earlier, Jane appears both weary and despondent and the life-story interview provided some insight on this in two areas. Firstly, shortly after the interviews, Jane's second major relationship ended amid much acrimony and, as has been characteristic, Jane left Citylimits High School. Secondly, Jane's identification of her own successes in teaching — and the problems she faces — are revealing. First, the successes:

I think when you have a successful team. That can make you feel, well, *pretty good*. But personally, I'll always remember [a pupil] who was pretty *uncoordinated* . . . and I used to encourage this girl as much as I possibly could in all the lessons, and she improved so much that *that* really made me feel on a high . . . As much as I can say that I've really felt good when my teams have won and things, sometimes, well, I think it comes down to individuals.

And the problems:

The main things that get *me* fed up with teaching are (long pause) the administration. And I really don't think that I actually get fed up with the teaching itself, I don't think I've ever really thought, *ever*, if I've been teaching: 'What am I doing here?' Sometimes I think 'this isn't as good as it should be' or, you know, 'better work to improve this next time' but it's not the teaching and I definitely go through phases, especially in the last couple of years, that all this new jargon and administration etc. is really too much and is really not for me . . . *that* makes me fed up. I mean, I know you shouldn't work in total isolation, I do realize that and I think I *could* work in total isolation (laughs) just get on with what I think is the right thing to do. I mean I do realize it but I just can't get along with all this *admin*.

Jane appears to use 'admin' as a generic term to refer to a plethora of initiatives which demand time she would rather devote directly to pupils. At the time of the interviews, the department had made very few changes in response to the National Curriculum, but the broader school community was embarking upon the formulation of some fairly extensive 'whole school policies' in a range of cross-curricular contexts. For Jane, her subject base is central to her role as a teacher: she seeks to provide pupils with fulfilment through physical education and sport just as she, herself, has achieved this end. She embraces initiatives which help her in this mission, as evidenced by her drive to introduce mixed gender physical education and health-related fitness components. Her underpinning view of sport is a broad one and she eschews any elitist approaches to teaching. The 'admin' which seems to cause the problem for Jane is that which resides outside her own subject department and which is a distraction from her perceived role: it is, to Jane, an irrelevance.

It would, perhaps, be simplistic to attribute Jane's stance to political naiveté. On the contrary, Jane made it clear that she was fully aware of the need to promote her subject within the school. She saw the introduction of mixed physical education, health-related fitness and examinations as positive steps in the battle to gain academic credibility for physical education.

However, Jane had no desire to progress up the hierarchy of school management as she wanted nothing that would take her away from the day-to-day immersion in physical education.

Another problem for Jane centres on her relationship with Pete, as was noted earlier. She views these difficulties as an example of personal failure:

> I'd really like to feel that the department was running smoothly and it isn't. I don't think I've been successful in that . . . it does worry me, you know, that I haven't really got a united department.

This was a recurring theme in our interviews and the importance of harmony within a department is mentioned by a number of the other teachers in this book. In this case it represents one of a series of problems and, as was indicated earlier, Jane's response to mounting pressures in both her personal and professional life was to change jobs. Her new post, since the interviews, in a college of further education, allows her to concentrate upon physical education almost exclusively. She is able to run examination courses at all levels, various sports awards and she can focus upon developing her subject in a less restrictive structure. This post would appear to offer Jane the opportunity to work in a way which *she* finds rewarding and it fits most aptly with her teaching philosophy.

In summary, Jane has made an assessment of her philosophy and that of the school and has rejected the latter. The desire to fight for her beliefs was tempered by her lack of ambition, particularly for career development in the broader school context. It is difficult to suggest how a school can more readily enhance the job satisfaction of someone like Jane. Unless she was to be allowed to continue in her preferred way, effectively isolated, some degree of discontent was almost inevitable. Given that analysis, the situation seems to have been resolved to the advantage of all.

Chapter 3

Pete

Pete is 45 years old and he has taught at Citylimits High School for 10 years. He is a keen sportsman and his personal mission, as a physical education teacher, is to encourage pupils to achieve high standards in sport. At one level he can be viewed, stereotypically, as a traditional, male physical education teacher given to severe bouts of sexism — but that would be an unfair parody. As with all stereotypes, the picture is far from simple. Pete's preferred image is one of 'tradition' and 'excellence' but his bravado masks disenchantment with a school system which he genuinely feels is failing pupils. He also believes the system has failed him in terms of recognition and promotion. Pete is often abrasive and he has refused to conform to, what he describes as 'educational bullshit'. His views may appear to be, at the very least, unfashionable: they are, nonetheless, thought-provoking.

As was noted in Jane's story in the last chapter, Pete tends to disagree with the other members of the physical education department at Citylimits High School. He has a particularly difficult relationship with Jane, for whom he has little respect. Some of this is fueled by his resentment of her position as head of department — a post for which he also applied. It could also be explained as just another example of his general approach to women but, here again, the picture is more complex than it first appears. It would certainly be fair to say that he tries to make life as difficult as possible for Jane and that the feelings, and the antagonism, are mutual.

Essentially, Pete's disenchantment stems from his belief that he has lost the battle to see his version of physical education legitimized. He would not, however, concede that he has lost the war as yet. In physical education, Pete looks for:

> Successful teams, successful individuals in individual sports. I firmly believe that this brings — it sets standards and it raises the less able to be better than less able. In comparison they'll always be less able than the top ones within the group but I think the overall standard will raise. Standards were far higher at this school when we pushed for more excellence.

Pete saw no reason to expect *all* pupils to achieve high standards in sport; as he put it, 'not everybody wants the same thing'. However, he saw it as his duty to ensure that those pupils with ability could achieve their full potential. Mixed ability teaching was, therefore, not a popular choice with Pete:

> What do you do in that situation? The educationists would say you have to teach the group. I say, that's what you're trying to do but you're failing. You're not really getting the cricket over to the people who are potentially cricketers and they're suffering because you're having to spend pro-rata more time on those who are totally disenchanted — well out of love with cricket . . . Be satisfied with those people who are not really going to *get it,* be satisfied with those people who are not going to reach a good standard and really get into those who you can perhaps see are going to make cricketers, and get some degree of excellence in a mixed ability group.

Pete seemed to be oblivious to the effect of this policy upon those who couldn't make the grade. On further probing, however, it became evident that he had based his comments upon what he considered were the practical realities of teaching. He was adamant that, in mixed ability groups, the more able pupils suffered: 'it's no good for them to do a good pass if the person at the other end has no concept of controlling it'. Such comments could easily be written off as the mutterings of an unskilled teacher. It could also be viewed as an honest statement on the very real difficulties experienced in teaching a broad band of ability in one group. None of the other teachers in the department endorsed Pete's views, yet observation of their lessons showed all faced similar difficulties. In many ways, Pete's remarks about mixed ability groups typify his approach to many issues: he is often insensitive — can even be offensive — and, unsurprisingly perhaps, his views are usually disregarded by the other teachers. However, his blunt and brutally honest expressions of frustration are born of an intense desire to focus on the detail of teaching at the mundane level of practicalities. Other members of the department were more willing to gloss over these local difficulties.

For Pete, then, physical education knowledge is, essentially, practical knowledge — sport. Health-related fitness was also endorsed as it coincided with his personal belief in 'the importance of staying fit and consequently healthy' — a view broadly shared by all the teachers in this study. Pete's emphasis on the 'practical' was reflected in his view of examinations in physical education:

> I'm not sure about that yet, I remember [a college lecturer] saying to me once that PE should be an alternative subject, alternative to exams. Playing sport should be enjoyable and you shouldn't have the pressures of exams, I don't know. I'm not sure about it yet.

His main concern with the GCSE examination was the breadth of the practical syllabus: 'you couldn't really *teach* them anything'. This is, perhaps, to be expected given Pete's overriding desire to teach pupils how to play specific games and do activities well. In the absence of persuasive and coherent arguments to the contrary, he will continue to see this as the core of all knowledge in physical education. For him, other claims for the educational value of physical education are nebulous, impossible to quantify and, perhaps more importantly, he sees no evidence of other teachers doing anything fundamentally different to himself. He may have a point. The most startling comment to be made about physical education lessons observed during the research at Citylimits, was their similarity!

Two other comments should be made about Pete's views on physical education. Firstly, he believes absolutely in the value of his subject as he sees it. But he is also an avid supporter of pupils in other areas of the curriculum where they are demonstrating the potential for excellence. He finds it difficult to accept, therefore, what he perceives as apathy towards sporting achievements amongst the rest of the staff: 'I used to say to one lady "get off your backside and get out, support them" because that same person was encouraging staff to gee them up in the classroom — the academic side — but how about the sports side?' Secondly, Pete feels strongly that a teacher must get to know a pupil to be an effective teacher. For him, getting to know the pupils is the foundation of teaching. He was unhappy with mixed sex physical education because of the lack of contact with pupils before and after lessons:

> I mean, you get to this time of year and you're writing reports for people and some of them I've hardly ever seen — *it's a farce* . . . I like to get relationships with the kids, you know, before the lesson starts, in the changing rooms, I'm disciplining, chatting, cheeking, you know, all the things that a teacher should do but half the class [in a mixed class] just walks into the sports hall. At the end of the lesson it's the same — 20 minutes of the lesson you are not talking to half the class. That's a major problem as far as I'm concerned.

The issue of mixed sex lessons arose repeatedly during the fieldwork at Citylimits, and an extract from fieldnotes is illustrative:

> [Pete asked for feedback on a mixed volleyball lesson observed earlier. I made the general comment that it was good that pupils were active and involved. He wanted more than that, so I mentioned the final game which I thought was far too large. This he accepted, and invited still further comment. I asked him who he considered to be the best player and, after some thought, he named a much favoured, cheeky and athletic boy. I pointed out that one girl in particular was far more skillful and controlled

and I suggested, from my perspective, that he expected far too little of the girls in the class — was not really prepared to challenge them in the way he challenged the boys. He felt this was possible and, in trying to work out why this was so, he put it down to (a) not *knowing* the girls and (b) being conscious of sexism so, perhaps, over-compensating in the 'wrong' way. He was very thoughtful on this issue and he confirmed what I had already noted during the lesson — that he had no difficulty identifying the needs of the less able girls, but had little idea how to deal with the able girls.]

Hence the comments made earlier, that although Pete can easily be classed as a traditional, sexist male physical education teacher, the picture is far from simple. Having spent time getting to know this individual, it was possible to appreciate some of the difficulties he was facing at a practical level.

Pete's theory of knowledge is similar to Jane's in that he sees a clear distinction between practical and theoretical knowledge. However, unlike Jane, Pete makes no apology for practical knowledge. He refuses to support, what he describes as 'the educationist perspective' which he views as damaging to his subject. His abrasive manner sometimes suggests a cynical and uncaring individual, particularly to those who don't share his views. However, although he may be cynical, he certainly cares — it's just that his particular concerns are rather unfashionable.

Looking back over Pete's life, there are some elements of his life-story which seem almost predictable given his reputation for sexism: for example, the relationship between his father and mother.

> My father was an electrician. (pause) Mother's always been a housewife. Father said 'you will never work'. (pause) I look back, I firmly believe that he implanted in my mind a lot of my values that I hold these days. Very much a dated outlook on the lady. Even in those days, I would say, I mean ladies did work in those days, although not so much in the country, more so in the city. But he would never allow mother to work, I always thought there was an element of distrust there. He was a very jealous man, I know that.

Pete described his father as 'very strict'. In contrast, his mother was 'the weak one — obviously you exploit that don't you?' He identified his grandmother and his older brother as the most influential people in his life. His grandmother is described as 'strong' and 'the most fantastic woman you'd ever wish to meet . . . a real character, a real extrovert'. Interestingly, it became clear that Pete's relationships with female colleagues was determined by his assessment of them as 'strong' or otherwise. Jane was considered to be rather 'weak' and therefore worthy of contempt.

Pete's brother has, perhaps, been the most important role model in Pete's life. Pete played all sports from a young age, but he never attained the same standards as his older brother: 'He was always regarded as better than me . . . a faster runner and better behaved. I was always in trouble.' Pete even described his talented brother as a 'big cross to carry' as he attempted to follow him through secondary school. His brother gained a place at teacher training college directly from school and Pete struggled to achieve that goal for many years.

In adult life, Pete has been married twice. The first marriage ended, partially because he decided to leave a job with his wife's family business to embark upon a physical education teacher training course, and partially because of conflict about Pete's sporting commitments. Upon reflection, however, sport was probably just the final straw. His second wife is described as 'more of a liberal lass' and 'very, very supportive'.

Pete identified his family, particularly his brother, as being far more significant as role models than any of the people he met through his school years. In making some brief comments about physical education teachers, Pete makes a clear distinction between the two approaches he encountered. The first was 'a *good man,* he helped kids out'. The second was more of a 'jack the lad . . . a big womaniser — he wasn't so dedicated'. The overriding influence in Pete's secondary school career was not a teacher but sport and its impact upon his academic work:

> It was all sport. I mean, it was the downfall of my education. I mean, I got to the fifth form and I ended up with two 'O' levels and in a grammar school, *that is bad.* That is *really bad.* It [returning to retake] was the most *degrading* thing I've ever had to experience . . . but I had to do it and *I worked like bugger* and as soon as I'd got them I buggered off!

A proud individual, Pete spoke with great feeling. Perhaps this is because he places such value on his position as a 'well known figure' — a position for which he seems to strive and for which sport is a vehicle.

Having left school and worked for 15 years, Pete decided that he really wanted to teach physical education, following in the footsteps of his idolized brother. At that point, as was noted earlier, his first marriage ended and he went to college as a mature student. On the whole he enjoyed the experience although it was tinged with some regrets:

> Yeh, *good times.* Wishing I was of student age . . . I didn't go to college at my prime in sport, and I felt that because I wasn't really competing with, uhm, college lads, I wasn't really doing *myself* credit. I was too old, basically, for the rugby side and cricket . . . I worked really hard on the education side. I studied like mad, not easy after you've had such a long break away . . . Basically very enjoyable. Only stayed for three years — long enough . . . Of the staff, X was excellent. Set standards. *No-one missed* X's lectures, *no-one* . . . X had a good old set of values which were not always there with other lecturers.

Upon leaving college, Pete obtained the post at Citylimits where he has remained since. Although he enjoyed an excellent relationship with a former headteacher, mutual dislike characterizes his relationship with the current head and he is now bitter and frustrated about his lack of career advancement. He feels that the whole senior management team is in opposition to his perception of how physical education 'should' be. He would describe himself as an innovator: for example, the introduction of the outdoor pursuits programme within the school and the development of both rugby and cricket within the local borough:

> I did *all these things* and I saw certain people (colleagues) who'd be wearing nice white shorts and nice this and that, being praised. I'd hear it from [the deputy head] how you should *project* the PE department and what he says is right in one way but, at the end of the day, who do you have — best teacher or best dressed one? Or one who doesn't create too many waves? There's no harm in waves you know. I've created waves. Some waves need to be created!

Clearly Pete feels that he is undervalued and he describes the 'high' and 'low' points of teaching in characteristic terms. Most of the successful moments are related to team and individual excellence in sport:

> . . . not just rugby but anything . . . because that is where I see a lot of hard work has been put in after school, which is of my own volition, no-one's forcing me to do it and that's where it really comes through. That's a high for me.

In contrast:

> Lows have been when (long pause) I've been stopped from getting to a high, getting promotion, having my own department. When I didn't get those jobs, all right, I *may* not have been the best one but (pause) I'm so conceited that I k*now* I was the best, I was the best, I really *know* I was the best . . .*I* gave the school a very high profile through sport and I say it, *I* did it.

Finally, Pete summarized his current position:

> A situation's been created here where I'm gonna stay at Citylimits as long as *I* want to. Citylimits School will not give me the mental kick that my other life gives me outside, 'cos my outside life, I am in full control of and that will stimulate me. I am in *full control* of that.

Pete's 'outside life' (what might be termed his 'side-bet', Becker, 1960) consists of a small, private old-people's home which he runs with his wife. Pete is proud of the risks he was prepared to take to establish this venture: 'I took things on, and I have always wanted kids to take things on and kids really appreciate that . . . I treat everything as a competition.' Importantly, the business has given Pete the economic freedom to make his own decisions about his future. It has freed him from the necessity of convincing others in the education system that his view of physical education has any merit. Like Jane, in the previous chapter, Pete has taken steps to alleviate the tensions between his personal philosophy of physical education, which centres largely on excellence in sport, and that of the school. Unlike Jane, however, Pete remains in post convinced that, in the long term, his view will prevail as schools seek to enhance their external image through sporting achievement. Pete has, therefore, neither changed his teaching philosophies nor his professional practice. He is, simply, waiting for his time to come.

Chapter 4

Arnold

Arnold is 36 years old and he has worked at Citylimits for 12 years. He has been head of boys' physical education but, in recent years, he has begun to move out of physical education and into careers and pastoral work. Arnold is quite different from Jane and Pete. He is highly regarded by other members of staff and by the senior management team. He is much more adept in the use of educational terminology than either of the other two and he would appear to hold a 'correct' educational philosophy — unlike Pete whose philosophy is most definitely 'incorrect'. One deputy head even described Arnold as 'intelligent' in comparison with Pete.

Interestingly, and in stark contrast to both Pete and Jane, Arnold appears to have very little enthusiasm for physical education. He devotes enormous amounts of time to careers and pastoral issues, to which he attaches increasing importance, and so he has little energy left for his main teaching subject. Paradoxically, he also expresses a high level of dissatisfaction with his job and he made it clear, on many occasions, that he is looking to 'get out' of teaching and has been doing so for several years. A certain despondency seems to characterize much of Arnold's thinking.

Arnold's comments about physical education focus on health and fitness, balance, and an holistic approach to teaching. For example, he summarizes the aim of the subject as follows:

> I think to promote a healthy lifestyle, yes, to also be able to direct individual skills to something fulfilling in terms of, er, a sport that they can take-up or follow; to be able to understand various sports that they come into contact with and to be able to improve their ability to be able to watch and take part.

He sees health and fitness as an increasingly important area but he's unhappy with what he considers to be a poor success rate:

> We've tried to encourage them to understand that we can't do it for them, that they have to take some responsibility for themselves and introduce them to some ways of doing it — er — and I think we fall down in some ways . . . tend to meet them in bars and pubs in a few years time and they're a gigantic size and not doing sport at all.

Arnold supports school clubs and sees much value in the existence of a 'school sport layer'. He places particular value on the concept of 'friendly rivalry' with other school teams and upon allowing 'kids to work with other kids from their own school'. He views physical education as 'a balance' between courses, teams, etc.:

> I think for most of our courses we are attempting to give them an idea of the skills involved in various sports, and our club facilities and our team games should be complimenting that for the ones that actually want to improve or go further and need coaching.

His view on examinations is more positive than Pete's, but is less enthusiastic — perhaps more pragmatic — than Jane's: 'We have got into examinations because it seems to justify our place a little more.' Perhaps the main difference between Arnold and the rest of the department is in his perception of his own teaching style. He teaches the same activities as his colleagues and his comments on the aims of the subject are also similar. He does, though, admit to a different philosophy of teaching:

> I've seen Jane teach and I've seen Pete teach and I think mine is a more holistic type of approach . . . obviously, Jane's is very much more skills based all the way through, probably more didactic as well. And I also try to use the reciprocal method of working, of helping each other and, er, everyone trying to spot each other's mistakes, that sort of thing — to improve their skills and to improve their relationships with others in the group, uhm, to be supportive of those who find it difficult, and I also think it does improve skills as well, and it improves their ability to be able to assess what's going on. Possibly you could look at it long term to the fact that they can actually appreciate sport when they view it.

Implicit in this is a perspective on knowledge in physical education which involves more than just content. It is probably a more articulate explanation of that which Jane described simply as 'it's more educational' and it suggests a specific concern with the social and moral development of pupils. Essentially, his views on teaching are warmly received in the school community leading one female colleague to comment: 'Arnold is better than most male teachers.' In particular, Arnold is perceived as being very different to Pete and, as Pete is viewed as a 'typical', male physical education teacher, so Arnold is viewed as 'atypical'. Taking all this into account, it could be expected that Arnold's lessons would be quite different in character and approach to those taught by other members of the department. In the event, however, this was not the case. An extract from fieldnotes on a mixed cricket lesson with Year 12 pupils is illustrative:

[Arnold gives a recap and some instructions — takes it very seriously — a fairly traditional start to the lesson. He rarely relaxes, uses little imagery, does not attempt to make it 'fun'. Sets up the second practice and this time reminds pupils to: 'tell your partner — see what they're doing. Tell him if he's doing it right. Constructive criticism please.' The pupils completely ignore this and get on with the activity. Arnold then draws them in and asks them to comment on their partner's performance. The pupils are unable to comment and seem confused by the question. I wonder if all this has been for my benefit as the pupils seem lost. (Arnold confirms this in a subsequent discussion.)]

Colleagues and senior teachers often drew comparisons between Arnold and Pete. As was noted in the last chapter, perhaps the most damaging charge levelled at Pete was that of sexism. However, Arnold was also sexist on a number of occasions: for example, in pushing the boys more in sports day trials; in labelling the girls' discus trial as 'a mother's meeting'; and in joking long and hard with a male physical education student about the girls' attempts in the 1500 metres. But, somehow, this didn't seem to count. The important point to be made is that Arnold is *perceived* by others as a 'better' teacher, perhaps because he can speak the approved language of education — a classic case, perhaps, of utilizing 'strategic rhetoric' (Sparkes, 1987).

Arnold accepts the fact that physical education is a low status subject and that it will get him nowhere in career terms. He feels that, in order to achieve promotion, he must obtain a further qualification — possibly a Masters degree — to prove he has 'academic knowledge'. His belief is that physical educationists are viewed as 'good disciplinarians' and 'good with kids' but not much else. Hence, perhaps, his air of despondency.

Arnold's life-story indicates that teaching was a natural choice of career. As the youngest brother of four sisters, two of whom became teachers, Arnold saw teaching as 'perfectly respectable'. Unlike Pete or Jane, there was no sporting influence emanating from his family; indeed, although Arnold's parents were very interested in his secondary school career, 'they were never, ever, able to watch any sports'. This was due, in the main, to their commitment to the family farm but their apparent lack of interest caused Arnold to feel resentful.

Although the decision to teach probably had its roots in his family, the choice of physical education was based entirely upon Arnold's experiences in the latter stages of secondary school. Up until this point, he had not encountered any positive role models in physical education: 'very unstructured lessons, it was very much "here's a ball, go on down and get yourself organized".' However, he represented the school at most sports, even though he describes himself as not particularly talented: 'It was such a small school it wasn't difficult to get into sides.' Arnold's belief that he has very little ability in sport was a consistent theme in all the interviews.

From what he described as 'a very regimented system in a grammar school', Arnold moved to a different sixth form, as a result of a local reorganization of schools. He relished the opportunities offered in the new school: 'a very free atmosphere . . . quite mind-blowing for us really.' In physical education, there was much more available and Arnold was able to become involved in a variety of new sports. In addition, he encountered what he describes as 'a *real* physical education teacher' for the first time:

> PE teachers there were very committed, very good sportsmen in their own right and it was there I met the first chap from X [teacher training] college. They were always available, lunchtimes and after school practices and that sort of thing. And extra-curricular activities were featured *high* on the school programme and they were very well thought of within the area and very well thought of, I believe, by the senior management at that school. I suppose, even at that time, I looked up to them as role modes, as I said, as *fit, committed people.*

Arnold did not take a conscious decision to teach as a result of his sixth form experience. Rather he chose to go to college as 'an enjoyable way to spend three or four years — to be involved in sport in that way'. Like the other teachers in this book, he describes higher education in enthusiastic terms:

> Oh (long pause) *whale of a time*! . . . we worked hard, enjoyed all the female company, er, representatively I played soccer when I was there for about three to four months. Wasn't very enamoured with the actual soccer situation at college, played at second team level only, I wasn't brilliant anyway but it was very much a rugby college, and rugby was the thing that was the social side of the college but, uhm, I probably would have played representative rugby there but I was deemed not good enough . . . *Very fond memories,* great teaching staff and lots and lots of good times . . . In fact they [the staff] were all such *outstanding* sports persons in their own right that I could never really look up to reaching that sort of level . . . from them all I think I've acquired a certain *professionalism* in dress and the way I approach kids and that sort of thing.

After leaving college, Arnold had great difficulty in obtaining a first teaching post. After 80 applications and 10 interviews he found supply work and, 'after three months of childminding' and a one-year contract, he was employed at Citylimits High School, where he has remained since. Although he has been head of boys' physical education, he has, as was noted earlier, made a conscious decision to move away from his physical education roots. Thus, it is, that he did not apply for the head of the new combined physical education department.

In his current role, Arnold is rarely in the staffroom and he has little contact with most of the teaching staff. As he commented: 'I used to be there. But now I'd be struggling to find anybody to talk to . . . I just haven't got *time.*' He also explained his evident lack of enthusiasm for physical education as, largely, a time problem. However, his responses to questions about high and low points in teaching are also revealing. First the 'highs':

> (long pause) No, I really don't think there is a time, well, maybe a few times when I taught English, when I thought I had a very successful lesson, it went very well, uhm, but I wouldn't have thought that any of my PE lessons were particularly — where I felt 'that was really good, that was — I achieved a great deal in that time'. There may have been a few pastoral situations where I may have felt that I did the right thing but *overall,* I don't know . . . I really couldn't pinpoint any particular time when I was successful.

And the low points:

> Oh, there's plenty of them, oh yeah. I think it's just the stress of actual amount of work, you feel you're just doing *too* much, and not able to be part of the staff . . . and you get to the point where somebody does something . . . then you just feel 'why bother?' . . . You think, 'there must be something better than this'. And obviously, getting home and doing more work and not living at all . . . I quite often get miserable or depressed . . . fed up with the teaching situation. Yeah, all the way through, right from when I started, there's always been an eye on the look out for something else, something more glamorous, attractive, with more money and less hassle . . . The whole problem with teaching is everything is attached to your teaching subject. If I could just have a pastoral role it would be OK.

Arnold's minimal interest in physical education is in sharp contrast to the positions of both Jane and Pete who have built their teaching careers around their perceptions of their subject base. Interestingly, Arnold appears to have less room for manouvre, in career terms, than either of the other two. He feels he should take a further qualification, as was noted earlier, but is not considering anything. Fundamentally, Arnold does not seem to have resolved the tension that exists between his teaching philosophy, the career moves which it suggests, and his niggling belief that he might — somewhere, somehow — be able to find 'something more glamorous'. He holds a view of physical education which extends beyond teaching pupils how to succeed in sport, but he gets little satisfaction from his endeavours to achieve this. Thus, it is, that he embarks upon no particular course of action and feels constrained in everything he does. It is difficult to see how Arnold can progress and begin to enjoy his job unless he can address this tension. He certainly feels that there is a 'system' which is preventing him from achieving his goals — and yet these goals are not identified clearly, even to Arnold himself.

Chapter 5

Diane

Diane is a recent addition to the department at Citylimits. She is now in her second year of teaching and is thoroughly enjoying her job. She feels comfortable in the department and she has a good working relationship with Jane, the head of department. Sikes (1988) noted that 'young physical education teachers tended to be strongly committed to their job' (p. 28) and this would be an apt summary of Diane. She is an enthusiastic supporter of new initiatives, she works hard and she has a 'grand plan' for her personal career development which she fully intends to implement.

Diane makes what, initially, appears to be a clear distinction between physical education and sport:

> I think there is a definite difference in that we are teaching them how to do the activities, and they are learning about their bodies, and how to use their minds as well, and all the social and emotional things that come into it. Whereas sport, I always see as out of school, they're just doing things — doing the activity, and so education is them learning about themselves and the activity, whereas sport — they're just doing it. I mean they do coincide in school, where they actually get into a game at the end and they actually do the activity — and, I suppose, in clubs. They are mutually beneficial, yes. The education side is obviously more intense, but then you learn anyway when you play sport — like to interact with other people and taking responsibility in, for example, a team.

For Diane, then, the important knowledge of physical education is not about the skills required to complete the activity successfully, but like Jane, it is learning about something else (in this case, themselves) and, like Arnold, there is a social dimension. So, when pupils play a specific game they are, essentially, learning how to work with others, with the execution of the activity itself viewed as of secondary importance. Diane was not particularly happy with her comments as she felt that she had contradicted herself and had missed something. However, she couldn't pinpoint it and, in the end, decided her explanation would have to do. Interestingly, the contradiction is borne out in many of her later comments.

Like others in the department, Diane feels that teams and clubs are important and that successful teams emanate from a strong curriculum. She sees it as essential to have a 'structured and organized syllabus' in order to present a good image within the school. In addition she views examinations in physical education as particularly valuable for the theoretical 'respectability' which they confer:

> It's good for the department to have an exam — it gives more status to teach it. If I moved on, I'd like the school to do it and if not I'd try and get it started. It doesn't bother me — the theory and all that. Some people at college didn't want to do it, but I really enjoy it.

Many of Diane's views are similar to those of Jane's and this probably explains their excellent working relationship. She also endorses Arnold's holistic approach to teaching although she wishes she could express herself as he does: 'If he says something I usually think — "I would have said that" or "I agree with that".' She has little time for Pete, although she agrees with his belief that 'knowing' the pupils is one of the keys to successful teaching. To this end, she involves herself in school trips with pupils from all years because 'it's good for them to see me as a person and not just a teacher'.

Centrally, Diane appears determined, focused and with a clear vision of her own goals. She believes that she should present an active and enthusiastic image if she wants success and promotion. Therefore it is important 'always to be very enthusiastic . . . always involved . . . In education as a whole, trying to get more involved with the pastoral work and also equal opportunities — I try and do lots of things.' Unsurprisingly, perhaps, her life-story provides numerous examples of this strength and clarity of purpose.

Diane's memories of her childhood are of a close, happy and somewhat extended family. She was close to her grandparents, cousins and, in particular, her older brother. Although there were no teacher role-models within the family, there was a high level of involvement in sport, notably with her mother: 'my parents, or my mum especially, was into lots of sports, and then with the school being good at it too, I got into it from there'. Reflecting upon primary school, Diane describes herself as 'a right goody goody' who always did well. Even at this stage of her life, Diane was heavily involved in various sporting activities through both the school and her family. At the end of primary school, Diane refused to take the scholarship examination for a local private school and, similarly, refused a place at a prestigious girls' church school. Her parents accepted her decision and she attended the comprehensive school of her choice.

Throughout secondary school, Diane was closely involved with the physical education department. She describes her physical education teachers in some detail:

> Oh they were brilliant! Absolutely brilliant. Jack, I suppose, was the one who had the *most* impact on me . . . he ran the ski trips every year and he was such a *nice person*, I mean, when I failed one of my exams he gave me a big hug as he was so upset for me . . . And Tracy, she was really good, she was so *loud*, so unlike anybody you've met before (laughs) and she was so down to earth and we sort of got on really well and she helped me a lot . . . Karen was a really good netball player, so she got our teams really going well, she was a good influence on my playing ability and, well, we were just really, really friendly and I could chat to them and go down and help them.

Diane had this depth of relationship only with physical education teachers; as she put it, 'just because of my interest in sport'. The strength of her sporting commitment is illustrated by her reaction to her perceived lack of ability in athletics: 'because I was no good at athletics, I used to take photos of sport instead'. The decision to become a teacher wasn't taken until Year 15, and was really quite accidental:

> We were having our PE. I was standing by the trampoline talking to some boy. He wanted to go to [a local teacher training college] and I thought: 'Oh yes, that's quite good' and, uhm, I like children, and I wanted to keep up my sport and I discussed it with my parents, and we came up with that.

Characteristically, Diane had made an assessment of her own ability and refused to take more than two 'A'levels: 'I knew I couldn't cope with three and I was right.' It was at this point, once the decision to teach had been taken, that one of the physical education teachers exerted a clear influence: 'she made me get all the prospectuses . . . and because she went to X college, she sort of pushed me in that direction. She was really nice and we still keep in touch.'

Diane loved higher education, and she still misses it. She describes her experiences with animation and enthusiasm:

> *Brilliant! Brilliant!* I miss it so much. Not necessarily doing the work (laughs) . . . but I miss *being there* . . . it's so nice to see people still from college . . . I would never, you know, *not* have gone and I would always say to somebody 'going away to university or college is for definite, you've just got to do it'. You learn so much about *yourself*, about other people, it's the time of your life. I mean, you work hard as well, or some people do — *I had to* (laughs).

Diane was successful in both academic and sporting contexts at college, and she still maintains regular contact with a number of her peers. She is now in her second year of teaching at Citylimits High School and, as was noted earlier, she enjoys her job. She describes the 'high' points of teaching in enthusiastic terms:

> In tennis, for example, all of a sudden they've [the pupils] *got it*. They've turned and done it properly and I've found myself shouting, *'Yeah, that's brilliant!'* . . . And when my team started to be successful this year . . . I could see they had potential, but it needed *a lot of work* and this year, all of a sudden, it clicked! . . . they won their section of the county tournament and went to the finals . . . and they won and they were *just over the moon* . . . and *that* was superb . . . it was such a good feeling to have a winning team that I'd worked with and they'd improved so much.

In stark comparison, low points in teaching centred around uncooperative pupils and Diane herself being in the wrong mood:

> . . . when they [pupils] are *so dim*, and some of them really are, and you can't get through to them and they show no signs of improvement whatsoever, and they don't seem to be trying. I find that really hard to motivate *myself* , let alone to motivate them. I find that *really frustrating*.

It is hard to summarize Diane's story. She appears to embrace many of the philosophies of the other teachers at Citylimits and, furthermore, she throws herself into broader school initiatives, particularly if they are likely to gain her some visibility within the school hierarchy. She is active in the construction of her career, and she gives the impression of someone who succeeds in the goals she sets for herself. For example, Diane applied for, and was awarded, one of the incentive allowances advertised internally. The allowance was for organizing bookings and other administrative duties relating to the school minibus. Although she would have preferred an allowance for physical education, Diane took the minibus incentive because 'I felt I had to get on an incentive this year, some way or other. I wouldn't have been happy staying on the main grade for another year'.

In terms of her development as a teacher, Diane commented that the most significant thing she has learnt about teaching so far, is that it is not necessary to 'put on an act' in front of pupils:

> I used to think you *had* to act if you were a teacher, it was some sort of acting role, but, being in it, I think I prefer myself, being myself with children. And I find they relate to somebody better if they know what you're like and they know that's the real you. I wouldn't feel secure. You know where you are if you're yourself.

Looking ahead, Diane prefers not to teach geography, her second subject, for at least another year. However, after that, she insists that any future post will have to offer the scope for some geography teaching so that she can broaden her career prospects. Arnold suggested that Diane's drive and enthusiasm are merely due to the fact that she is 'early into the system' and that she will, inevitably, 'become worn out with the system or beaten by it'. Although this has been Arnold's experience, Diane appears to manage the education system confidently — even effortlessly. Her self-belief may carry her through.

Enterprise High School

Enterprise High School is a multi-racial secondary school, located in the centre of a major city. It is, in all respects, an 'inner-city' school, with a student population approaching 900. The school has good sporting facilities, including two gymnasiums and a sports hall. However, the absence of on-site fields is viewed as a problem by the physical education staff, with many departmental activities having to take place at a location a little over two miles away.

The physical education department consists of three members of staff: Laura is the ebullient head of department, Edgar is the second member of staff who has recently spent some time as acting head of department, and Liz. The staff perceive the school's senior management team to be very supportive of them and their efforts. This is particularly appreciated by Laura, who has found previous schools to be considerably less supportive.

The department is heavily committed to running extra-curricular sports clubs for the pupils, both during the lunch hours and after school. This would appear to be a source of tension between departmental staff. Laura appears very much to be the driving force behind the department and its activities, with its varied intra- and extra-curricular programme reflecting her enthusiasm to succeed at the job. The success of the school sporting teams is also very important to all staff, and to Laura and Edgar in particular. This reflects a departmental belief in the importance of projecting a 'winning' image for the school. They also believe in the wider, personal benefits that sporting participation can bring.

At the time of interviewing, Edgar had just resigned from Enterprise High, citing the pressures of dealing with unruly pupils and an increased teaching and administrative load as the primary reasons. Both Laura's and Edgar's stories are told in the next two chapters.

Chapter 6

Laura

Laura is a lively, ambitious 29-year-old, and is head of department at Enterprise High School. This is her second teaching post, which she has held for the past four years. Although not as active as she once was, Laura is a keen sportswoman whose enthusiasm for her subject, and for sport in general, is obvious. Her commitment to her teaching role, and all that it entails, is clearly evident. However, the pace at which she runs the department, including the level of sustained commitment she expects from her staff, is beginning to result in signs of strain and tension.

Despite Laura's love of sport and her acknowledgment of its impact upon her career, she identifies wider socio-psychological benefits to pupils as the main purpose of physical education:

> I see my role and the role of my subject as to enhance their [pupils'] self-esteem . . . to make them feel like they've got something to offer be it individually or in a group . . . it's preparing them for the world beyond and that they would feel comfortable in approaching any sporting environment.

Giving pupils a 'worthwhile' experience is very important to Laura and she expresses the belief, enthusiastically, in a number of different ways: 'filling them with confidence', 'it's giving them . . . a love of something'. Laura also believes that physical education must be enjoyable, and perceiving that pupils enjoy her subject far more than others is obviously a source of immense personal pride. Although she acknowledges that this enjoyment is largely due to the *physical* nature of the subject — 'they're doing physical activity, they just love it' — she still insists upon the value of social and socio-psychological benefits, rather than seeing participation in sport as valuable in its own right.

Laura's commitment to her profession — her passion — is clearly evident when she discusses her job:

> I believe that we are there to do a job . . . although it's not just a job, it's more than a job. If a teacher is not really into the job and becomes dis-illusioned, then the kids just switch off. Its a vocation — no-one can be

trained to be a PE teacher — well, you can train them , yes, you can do the theory and all that, but being teacher, no matter what subject it is, is in-built in you and you've either got it or you haven't.

In fact, enthusiasm, concern and devotion characterize all Laura's comments as she considers her role as head of department and outlines standards she sets for herself and others. For example, in seeking to distinguish between physical education and sport, Laura is thoughtful, yet certain that they are completely different. When she teaches physical education, and what differentiates her from a coach, is the way 'she handles her subject'. Thus, Laura's focus is upon the pupils, not the sporting activity. Her philosophy is more complex, however, in that within a child-centred framework, Laura strives for maximum pupil participation in sport, but also believes firmly in providing extra opportunities for the more talented to excel. She would view this as giving pupils the best of both worlds. In developing her thoughts further, Laura suggests that one of the aims of her department is 'excellence', and this explains the departmental policy of 'buying in' coaches for certain sports. The difference between herself, as a teacher, and the coaches, is thus explained mainly in terms of breadth of task:

> If you get some one in that's purely football focused or purely basketball focused, then they're purely focused on their sport. They are focused on being the best lay-up merchant, the best free-throw merchant, whatever . . . whereas when I'm educating, I'm not isolating one or certain members of the groups, as I'm educating to a whole range of pupils and so that all pupils will achieve.

Laura, therefore, sees her teacher-role as being largely generic in nature, rather than teaching specific activities such as sports. However, she recognizes the inevitable paradox in trying to combine the twin aims of maximum pupil participation on the one hand, and making special provision for the more talented pupils on the other. Furthermore, the employment of sports coaches in the department reflects a recent revision in her philosophy for physical education: she now believes, somewhat reluctantly in the light of the current political climate, that sport education, as opposed to physical education, is where the future of her subject lies. In summary, a philosophy in flux.

Laura's evolving philosophy is confirmed again in her comments about teaching mixed ability and, particularly, mixed gender groups. She has changed her original views as a result of the problems she now believes to be inherent in such groupings. Her overriding aim is to provide quality physical education experiences for all, and as much as possible, to meet the needs of every individual child. Hence, she believes changes must be made:

> I was personally a great advocate of mixed ability and mixed gender teach-
> ing four or five years ago, it was the Bible, because I used to think that
> single-sex teaching was something that was done in the 60s, something that
> the previous generation did, and I firmly believed that single sex (teaching)
> didn't work. I actually now feel that . . . ummm . . . my whole philosophy
> is changing, and I don't know if that's good or bad. [Interviewer : why?]
> 'Cos suddenly, day-in, day-out I'm faced with situations where maybe girls
> are embarrassed or often the boys make them feel uncomfortable so they
> stop participating. And when I say that I'm aiming for maximum participa-
> tion , that's what I'm aiming for, so that maybe one of the reasons why
> we're separating the girls out.

In perceiving the boys to be dominant in the games lessons, to the detriment
of the girls, Laura faced a challenge. She knew the situation was untenable,
given her firm views on maximum participation for all and, as a result, the
department is now implementing single-sex lessons in Years 8–10. All
members of the department view the initiative as a success.

In the context of the wider school community, it is clear that Laura and
her department are valued highly. However, although Laura describes the
management of the school as 'very supportive' she still considers that physical education 'gets a bad rap' from other teachers. She puts this down to
the fact that 'the old phys edder, sweaty jock' stereotype is very much alive
within the staffroom. She does see a slow change in this attitude, particularly
as physical education becomes more 'academic' and physical education
teachers present a better image: 'academically, we've proven that we're a
subject to be reckoned with'. However, she also feels that any increase in
respect is the result of changes in image, rather than in substance.

At a personal level, Laura retains a strong belief that physical education provides an excellent environment in which to establish meaningful
relationships with pupils:

> At the end of the day, we're dealing with a lot of children who don't trust
> anyone. One of the best pieces of advice I was ever given was from the
> deputy head at my last school, and he said 'Laura, in these children's lives,
> we're some of the most constant things. They know in the morning when
> they come in that you will still be there for them, whereas when they go
> home at night they don't know what's happening'.

Laura views the physical education environment as something very unique,
where considerable potential exists to overcome traditional teacher–pupil
barriers. She works hard to build relationships with individual pupils; to
help them to reach their full potential. Laura undoubtedly *cares* for her
pupils:

Children know whether you care, they know whether you're interested. If you're interested in them, they're interested in your subject. When they get to Key Stage 4, when they're choosing their options, they'll think who's taught them before. The philosophy is within the children.

She sees extra-curricular time as particularly valuable in the task of relationship building. Herein lies Laura's justification for the staff time and energy which is devoted to the extensive extra-curricular programme at Enterprise High. She has great respect for the potential of, what might be termed, 'the sporting environment' in an educational framework. Physical education is, then, the context within which sport can be harnessed for the benefit of pupils and Laura's role is to make sure that it happens.

Laura's interest and belief in sport were fostered from a very early age. Both parents were active sports people, with her father being a former physical education teacher. She excelled in a number of sports during her school years, becoming an international track and field athlete. Her supportive family background, and obvious love of sport, more than compensated for some negative physical education experiences at secondary school. She recognizes, however, that many of her school friends were 'turned-off' the subject by an uncaring, apathetic teacher and the experience has had a profound effect on Laura's philosophy as a teacher. At the very least, Laura strives to be the antithesis of her own teacher, recognizing that she can be significant and influential in pupils' lives. This means that the role demands unswerving commitment and endless enthusiasm from anyone who enters the profession. Laura will tolerate no less.

Why do you think, I am like I am in wanting my children to achieve. That's part of my philosophy . . . it's the reason why I am like I am, I want everyone to achieve. I want those who have got potential to really achieve their full potential. What happened to a lot of children I went to school with was that the teacher didn't really care, so they stopped caring. We had to fix up our own fixtures, and we had to bully the teacher to go with us to the fixtures. I don't ever want that to happen, and the minute that starts happening to me in teaching, I'm getting out or I'm getting into another area of the job. When I've lost my enthusiasm and dedication, then that'll happen.

Laura admits that a physical education teacher is all she ever really wanted to be. Her university years, which she entered straight from secondary school, are remembered with many smiles: 'When I got there, I had the time of my life.' She enjoyed all the practical lectures, but didn't really get the most from the sports clubs: 'my experience at college . . . with athletics, I didn't train as much . . . I played hockey, but I didn't like the cliqueness of things like the clubs.' Nevertheless, Laura retains many fond memories of her university days, and particularly of the department in which she was trained. Again, however, it was the social side of sporting involvement that emerged as the most important. Sport was the vehicle that allowed her to develop good relationships with both staff and students and to gain increasing self-confidence.

Now she is teaching, and leading her own department, Laura is aware that her level of commitment can be rather intimidating for colleagues. She is also aware that she has a dominating influence over the department. She views this, however, as an indication of the shortcomings of others; particularly new teachers, who appear unwilling to offer views and ideas on curriculum or departmental matters. Furthermore, as was noted earlier, the extent of her enthusiasm for extra-curricular activity, and the demands she makes on colleagues' time, have resulted in tension between herself and her staff. Unperturbed, Laura powers on, revelling in the support offered by the headteacher and determined that her subject will be successful:

> I'm in a situation where sometimes I have to pinch myself because my head is so supportive. The other staff sometimes get pissed off because it's always the PE department who get stuff, or it's the PE who have done this or that. Children get to know about the school through the publicity we get, and children then want to come to the school. I've got children to be representing GB, so the profile of the school is raised. The head wants my subject to work.

Laura's thoughts on her own future, in many ways, reflect her career to date. Although ambitious, her principal source of enjoyment in the job comes from working closely with pupils and establishing rewarding relationships with them. She acknowledges the potential for such an emotional and energetic investment in pupils to take its toll and, at the moment, she is feeling a need to ease off a little, and enjoy the job as it is:

> The future for me and my career? I'm hoping to get deputy head status ... but I'm not going to put a time schedule on myself though. I did think I was moving a bit too fast, and someone said to me, 'Laura you'll be a deputy by the time you're 30 so what are you going to do after that?' So I thought, 'Yeah, why am I in such a rush?' I'm aware that I've achieved a lot very quickly, and I give a lot of myself to my subject ... but the higher up you go, the more distance you get from the children. I'll get there, but now I'm prepared to give it just a little bit more time because I'm still enjoying what I'm doing and I'd miss it. I'd miss the contact with the department and working with people ... the higher up you get, it becomes a 'them and us'. It's in the future though. It doesn't mean that I'm not ambitious for myself, but right now, I just want to enjoy my job.

The concept of caring for the children as individuals is a constantly recurring theme in Laura's story. She is aware of the social and psychological benefits sporting involvement gave her, and is determined to offer similar opportunities to her pupils. She considers her strengths to be 'the ability to get on with people, especially young people', and her involvement in sport. She believes that she has found the ideal job for her: 'I know that . . . umm, God this sounds so unrealistic like I'm searching for utopia, but I know I can make a difference.' Her drive and passion for her job are unquestionable; this is both her strength and her weakness.

Laura's Comments about her Story

At first glance I come across as a teacher who is obsessed with the social side of physical education. In the pursuit of excellence and optimal participation, my approach to teaching a range of activities is to aim for quality of performance and experience for all. By 'buying in' outside coaches for extra-curricular activities it also enables us to offer an even broader programme to cater for even more pupils' needs.

It may appear that I see the extra-curricular programme as a major focus of the pupils' physical education experience, however, there is no value in such a programme if they [pupils] do not experience a well-planned and educative curriculum at Key Stages 3 and 4.

Chapter 7

Edgar

Edgar is 31, and has taught for three years. His story contrasts sharply with that of Laura, particularly in the amount of *himself* that he is willing to invest in his job. He entered teaching late, having left school with few qualifications. He then spent a number of years working as an audio-visual technician. It was disillusionment with his career progress that led him to consider the possibility of entering higher education to gain a teaching qualification. The idea to train for physical education teaching stemmed from his love of sport and enjoyment of coaching football, a sport which he continues to play at a good semi-professional level.

Edgar gained access to a BEd course through a preceding sub-degree qualification. The post at Enterprise High School is his first since leaving university. Recently, he was promoted to acting head of the physical education department because Laura was made temporary head of year. Initially, he was very enthusiastic about the promotion but, in the event, relationships in the department became strained and this caused some personal difficulty for Edgar. The problems originated not only from the third member of staff, Liz, who was overlooked for the post, but also from the fact that Laura was still working in the department and was, therefore, answerable to Edgar as the acting head.

Although only having three years' teaching experience, Edgar's enthusiasm for the job has declined markedly in the last six months. This is due, in part, to his perception of an increase in the administrative load of teaching. More importantly, perhaps, he views the unruly behaviour of many of the pupils at Enterprise High to be completely unacceptable. In combination, these issues prompted his recent decision to resign. At the time of our interviews, Edgar had just left Enterprise High and was working as a supply teacher in the primary sector.

Edgar's personal philosophy of physical education focuses on the centrality of *education*. He is particularly keen, for example, to emphasize the role of physical education in providing opportunities for the less academically talented to express themselves and excel within the curriculum:

> PE itself though has its own importance, in that it gives the less academic
> kids a chance to shine at something. I think PE can also raise the confidence

54

of kids, especially those who aren't really academic, and not respected in
any other subject. Yeah . . . it's definitely an area for self-expression and
to develop feelings of self-worth and self-confidence.

He believes that children should be given equal opportunities and equal
access to a wide range of differing experiences in school — thus, his belief
in offering a large number of sports within physical education lessons.
Edgar also values his subject for the preparation sport can give pupils for
life. In particular, he sees team games as having the potential to develop
cooperative and other social skills in children. Additionally, he believes
that a 'good' physical education teacher should aim to encourage students
to have a life-long interest in sport and physical activity, thus giving them
the opportunity to be fit and healthy. Consequently, although still a keen
and active sportsman who plays football at a serious level, Edgar's beliefs
about the value of sport for pupils seem to focus more readily upon social
development and health education. This represents a shift from his original
philosophy, in which he valued the sporting experience for its own sake; a
belief that was instrumental in his initial decision to become a physical
education teacher.

In describing a successful physical education department, Edgar again
highlights the importance of the development of social values. Thus, he sees
physical education as:

> Something that's interesting, challenging, creative and progressive. The
> kids should be pushed individually, so there should be a system of indi-
> vidual differentiation between the kids. We should really try to incorporate
> the social aspect a lot more in that we, and the subject, should help kids
> understand that they need others to get on in life. The games should be
> conditioned for maximum involvement.

In relation to his personal teaching philosophy Edgar, like Laura, considers
the establishment and development of good relationships with pupils as
being of paramount importance. However, unlike Laura, his personal experience in this respect has been largely negative. He raised the issue of staff–
student relationships, and in particular the subject of discipline and respect,
at several points in the interviews. Indeed, it was the constant battle with
pupils to establish, what Edgar views as 'appropriate' relationships, that
ultimately proved one of the primary factors in Edgar's decision to leave
Enterprise High:

> Before you can have a good rapport with the kids, you have to get their
> respect. The respect has to be gained in different ways from different
> kids. At the start you need to be firm, but not too firm. For example with

> inner-city kids, if you shout at them, they just switch off, where with kids
> that are not so streetwise you can shout at them and get some fear-type
> respect. I guess it's a mixture of fear-type respect, and respect for your
> knowledge that you're really aiming for.

Although he is secure on the theory, in reality Edgar finds the behaviour of
pupils at Enterprise High to be intolerable. His family background, where
respect and courtesy were the norm, contrasted sharply with the situation at
Enterprise High and he found the constant battle to maintain the respect of,
and discipline over, pupils very wearying. From his earliest days at Enterprise High, Edgar became aware that this might be a problem. Interestingly,
in his initial 'honeymoon period' at the school, he was more inclined to view
the pupils as lovable rogues: 'You need to keep ahead of them — they don't
half keep you on your toes!' However, when describing the final weeks of
his job, any spark of enthusiasm had been extinguished by disillusionment
with pupils' behaviour. Furthermore, he feels that he was often called upon
to deal with the most difficult pupils that other staff couldn't handle, perhaps
because of his imposing 6' 3" frame, or possibly just because of his physical education background. To add to Edgar's difficulties, he was asked to
take, what he perceived as, a particularly difficult form class in his second
year at Enterprise High, and this fed his growing resentment of the daily
struggle with unruly pupils.

It was also during this period that Edgar was promoted to acting head
of department, in preference to Liz, when Laura was offered temporary
promotion to head of year. Although, initially, Edgar relished the additional
responsibility, there was an accompanying increase in his administrative
workload. Furthermore, tensions became evident because of his altered relationship with Liz and, particularly, with Laura who remained within the
department, and this became very stressful for Edgar. Perhaps as a result
of these pressures, Edgar began to resent the time that he was expected to
devote to extra-curricular activity:

> I think the only thing I really disagreed with Laura about was on the kids
> involvement with the sports clubs. I'd have cut down on the lunchtime
> clubs, as we ended up having to do three a week! As a teacher, I think we
> need a break from the kids. I never had any arguments with her (Laura),
> but the lunchtime clubs thing was no good. Sometimes I'd be eating my
> lunch as I'm taking the club . . . God, I was getting indigestion! The whole
> thing would just go on and on, and we'd never get a proper lunch . . . it got
> me down a bit.

Not that it was all conflict. The department reached unanimous agreement
on single-sex teaching, for example, and Edgar, in particular, saw this as an

essential step in keeping pupils on-task and interested in the lessons. He wished that the policy could have been extended to all year groups.

Although he considered the head of Enterprise School to be very supportive of the physical education department, Edgar perceived some hostility and a condescending attitude to the subject among other staff: 'I know some of them [teachers] think of PE as just a chance for the kids to let off some steam before they got back to some "real" work.' The principal bone of contention for Edgar, however, was that other staff would sometimes use physical education as a punishment:

> ... they'd exclude kids from the sports teams (as a punishment for misbehaviour). Some teachers would come up to me and say that they didn't want so-and-so kid to play on a sports team. That really caused friction between us and other departments ... I'd get pissed off if some of the football team were in detention and missed a game, 'cos I think that other staff used that against the kids, like saying if you don't behave you're going to miss that game, just 'cos they couldn't control the kids. I found that really unfair.

Given Edgar's personal love of sport, it is unsurprising that he finds the views and actions of his colleagues unacceptable. Sport, and particularly football, have been of great importance to Edgar. However, although coming from a very close knit and supportive family, parental encouragement for his sporting involvement was, and still is, minimal:

> Mum always wanted me to play the piano, not to do sport. She wasn't too keen on football at all, just wanted me to become a teacher, but not a PE teacher! I think it's a West Indian thing really ... parents emphasize the academic side and not the sporting side, 'cos I've got mates who say the same thing. Dad didn't say much to push me into either academics or sport, although he was concerned for me to get a good education ... He certainly didn't want me to work outside as a painter like him, although he's never said it, I certainly feel it.

Edgar's physical education experiences at school were mixed. Although generally enjoying the activity, he never envisaged himself as a physical education teacher because, even at that stage, he found the attitude and behaviour of some of his peers disturbing: 'I do remember thinking I'd love to do this [be a physical education teacher] all day, but I always thought I'd never be able to handle the nutters.' It is, perhaps, unsurprising therefore, that one of the principal reasons for Edgar's recent decision to leave Enterprise High was poor pupil discipline and lack of respect for teachers.

Edgar left school at 17, and worked for a few years as an audio-visual technician. Simultaneously, he played semi-professional soccer in London, whilst also spending two summers as a professional footballer in Sweden. Having decided that his career was going nowhere, Edgar finally responded, almost reluctantly, to a friend's suggestion that he go to college and perhaps become a teacher. He was 24 when he took up the challenge.

> Anyway, he [a friend] sent me a university prospectus, and I applied half-laughingly only to satisfy my mum really. I remember going for the interview where we had to design our own dance to the Pink Panther music! I got through it (laughs). We had to do a bit of coaching as well . . . I was really nervous. About a week later, I got a letter offering me a place and I had to let them know within two weeks. I remember speaking to a friend who said that I could do it, but I still wasn't sure . . . I guess I was trying to find excuses not to do it. Anyway, I went to County Hall to apply for a grant, half hoping that they wouldn't give it to me. But I got a very good grant, 'cos I had been working for the local authority, so I decided to go!

Edgar's initial anxiety about his suitability as a university student extended through much of his course. Because of his 'weak academic background', he feels that he had to work harder than most to produce written work of the required standard. He was not involved in university club sport because of his contract with a semi-professional football club. This, however, is not something he particularly regrets, as he took his commitment to his club very seriously, although he is aware that perhaps this is one aspect of college life on which he missed out. Otherwise, Edgar undoubtedly considers college as a great life experience and one upon which he reflects with fondness.

Following graduation, Edgar had little difficulty in finding a job and his first post was at Enterprise High. He can identify 'highs' within the job, particularly an enthusiastic first year of teaching, and his appointment as acting head of the physical education department, which he views as a considerable achievement. However, he finds it much easier to articulate the low points: his perception of a significantly increased teaching and administrative load, continuing problems of pupil discipline and respect, and the burdensome involvement in extra-curricular activities. In combination, these factors sapped Edgar's early enthusiasm and led to his ultimate resignation. Although he reflects on his time at Enterprise High as a very valuable and, to an extent, an enjoyable learning experience, he feels that, as a new teacher, he was not given enough support and that his workload was unfair. Thus, Edgar's desire to be a physical education teacher has been replaced by frustration and a little anger. He feels that resigning was the only option to escape a draining situation.

Edgar is currently working as a supply teacher in the primary school sector. He has no regrets about leaving Enterprise High, and appears to want to enter the secondary sector again when the 'right' job comes up.

> I'm optimistic that I'll get the *TES* (*Times Educational Supplement*) in September and find a job that I want to do in a good school and start at Christmas. I still really want to work in PE, but I really needed the rest, 'cos without it I'd have been physically and mentally knackered. It took me a long time to unwind once I'd left Enterprise.

Whether he finds it easier elsewhere, remains to be seen.

Edgar read his story but chose not to add any further comments.

Two Teachers, Two Schools

Maggie and Grant teach in very different schools, although both have a wide range of teaching experience. Maggie's first post was in a grant maintained girls' school, but she now teaches in a mixed comprehensive with limited facilities for physical education and little management support for her subject. Her pupils are challenging both in terms of discipline and motivation. Grant, on the other hand, started his teaching career in mixed comprehensive schools, with numerous social and discipline problems, but now teaches in a boys' grammar school. Here, the intake is academically selective, facilities at the school are good, staff and senior teachers are enthusiastic about the role of physical education and the pupils are keen and able. Comparing the two, it would appear that Maggie and Grant have taken different routes in their teaching careers, yet their stories are linked by an indefatigable commitment to physical education.

Chapter 8

Maggie

Maggie is a positive, reflective and talented teacher. She is 28 years old and is thoroughly committed to a career within secondary education. She has an infectious enthusiasm for teaching and for physical education, believing firmly that participation in sport offers pupils unrivalled opportunities for personal development. Maggie is currently head of girls' physical education in a mixed comprehensive school. She is also studying, part time, for a Masters degree in Education. She admits to being uncertain about her next career move, but her personal experience of a rather haphazard system of Continuing Professional Development has stimulated her interest in conducting some form of research in this area.

Maggie's story is characterized by a driving ambition to ensure that pupils can benefit from sport, just as she believes she did. Thus it is, that she has come to reject some of the philosophies she encountered — and espoused — at teacher training college. The significance of the National Curriculum is underplayed — 'it's just gone on to confirm what people have already done in good practice in PE', and although she realizes that the status of being within a National Curriculum subject is important — 'it is a framework rather than a bible'. Maggie is developing a new teaching philosophy based on the realities of teaching: 'the more I teach, the more I think what is lacking in kids is some of the basics'. Her reasoning for this is that pupils need more basic skills in order to access the range of sports activities and the resulting personal development 'spin-offs':

> I used to think I was going to change the world and it's gone full cycle and I feel now that I want more and more to concentrate on achieving the basics; building from there . . . so although at college I was very keen on the games for understanding approach and, experimented a lot with that and in fact used that quite a lot, I find that sometimes I do have to go back to this business of basics . . . I think that the more I teach the more I see the necessity for it for them to access other areas.

Thus it is, that Maggie has narrowed her original aims and now seeks to focus upon: '*physical* education and I think that's what we've got to concentrate on and our job is improving performance through movement . . .

I think maybe we try to do too much sometimes'. She views gymnastics as a foundation for all sporting activities and is seeking to elevate its status in her own department. Health education is also important for Maggie — but she is interested in trying to improve fitness, which she perceives to be at worryingly low levels, rather than just seeking to improve pupils' *understanding* of fitness principles. She understands the difficulties in achieving this, particularly in the time given, but still looks to see definite, measurable achievements: 'we need to perhaps, initially, not be as broad in our intentions, even if it can only be in understanding the whys of health'.

Liaison with primary schools is perceived, by Maggie, to be a particular problem. As she points out, other subject areas set tests for primary pupils so that the teachers have information upon which to develop their Year 7 curricula. In physical education 'what we do is launch into a programme of activity and we really don't know what the starting point is'. Maggie would question, therefore, whether her curriculum is 'child-centred' at all and sees a need for some form of test to identify the pupils' starting points: 'I often think we find out too late the areas of weakness and we could be making progress much quicker if we analysed it to begin with instead of looking at it when it's all too late.'

Maggie is, as was noted earlier, a reflective teacher. It is, perhaps, to be expected, that she sees communication, reflection and critical analysis as central to a successful physical education department:

> . . . there are so many changes that happen in the PE department that it's really important to find slots to sit down and decide some sort of group philosophy, a group direction with room for individual teaching styles and strategies . . . I don't think we sit down as professionals enough to *discuss, share* our experiences. I don't think you necessarily have to completely share the same aims but I think you've got to be prepared to sit down and communicate with each other on the things that you disagree or agree with and *try things out*.

For Maggie, the successful department helps pupils to improve their skills in the specific activities, but does more also. She believes that pupils should be enthused to participate after school and out of school, and hopes that some will even want to go on to teach and coach themselves. Furthermore, extra-curricular activities are seen as, potentially, a rich source of education: 'I think I go back to my own experiences sometimes, to think about what I'm doing now and, definitely, part of my education in life, not just about sport, was a result of being involved in teams.' Here again, Maggie finds that she has changed some of her earlier views: 'I used to have these grand ideas about not giving too much emphasis to school teams but the more I teach, the more I see the value of it.' She is able to recount numerous stories of disaffected pupils who have matured and have found some meaning and purpose in school through participation in sport. She is proud of those successes, if a little apologetic. It seems that some small part of Maggie still believes that, in spite of her experience, she really ought to espouse more of her teacher training philosophies. She points out, for example, that although she has tried to utilize — and still values — a 'games for understanding' approach where pupils create games to learn game concepts, she is increasingly finding that a skills-based approach is more effective for the pupils: 'I *do want* the best for the kids and I think that you've got to be prepared to use the best method regardless of whether it's on the right bandwagon at the time.' The tension in Maggie's thoughts emerges again towards the end of this story when she identifies extra-curricular involvement as *the* high point of teaching.

In attempting to identify a distinction between physical education and sport, Maggie was sure that a difference existed, but has some difficulty articulating her thoughts. She feels that in physical education 'we are *teaching sport*, but we're using [that sport] as a vehicle to open up a lot of other avenues'. For example, 'a lot of the things that apply in netball they can apply elsewhere, not just in games, but they can apply elsewhere in their life as well.' Again, this would appear to be based on her own experience of sports participation: 'it's education through sport . . . I know the value of sport myself, as a form of education, because I've gone through that'. After much further deliberation, Maggie summarized her position as follows:

> . . . there are some general principles in netball that apply in other sports, so you'd use catching and throwing and shooting which then apply in basketball. There are things that apply in netball, basketball, that then apply in all sports — etiquette, safety, health. But then you expand it even further and it then becomes (long pause) a social attitude that by relating to people in a sporting context, you learn how to relate to people in life, in general.

Given this staged approach, the rationale for Maggie's 'back to basics' philosophy becomes clearer. She has decided that 'in order for pupils to learn though netball, they've got to be able to achieve some basic levels of performance'. Furthermore, our lengthy conversation on the sport/physical education interface took an unexpected turn as Maggie suddenly asked: 'Why do we call it physical education anyway?' She made the point that, in schools, the terms 'maths education' and 'science education' are not commonly used. After much thought she concluded: 'I think it's because we just have to try and justify ourselves beyond the public's image of sport being for the elite . . . in schools there's no other subject area that has to use the word "education" to justify itself.' In the end, Maggie thought 'physical, sport and health education' would make a much more accurate subject title.

Maggie had no idea what the senior management team thought of her department, her subject or her teaching in either of her two posts. In her first post she had no communication with the headteacher at all. In her current post she feels that communication would be possible: 'but I feel really guilty approaching him because he's so busy'. In an interesting parallel to Grant's story, the only issue upon which any detailed communication has occurred is sports day, where a clash of philosophies about the purpose of the event emerged.

Maggie's belief in the value of participation in sport can be traced back to a thoroughly sports-oriented childhood. She comes from a family of eight children and, although her parents were not actively involved in sport, two of her older sisters were a major influence upon her. One sister, for example, took Maggie to a gymnastics club each week, even though this involved a lengthy bus journey. Maggie's belief in the fundamental importance of gymnastics skills as a general body training activity is thus explained:

> It was the *first* thing which gave me the grounding, in terms of strength, suppleness and speed — not so much stamina — but it gave me a good grounding to be able to develop in lots of other areas so I'm a real firm believer now in kids doing gymnastics to give them access to other sports.

In addition to her own large family, the family next door consisted of eleven children and this, too, was central to Maggie's involvement in childhood sport: 'Obviously they had kids exactly the same age as all of us, so we had a great deal of competition between the families and we competed at *everything*.' Maggie recalls that she was always playing one form of sport or another, either with her own family or her neighbours. It is a period of her life upon which she enjoyed reflecting: 'I loved it, absolutely loved it. *Really happy memories*.' She also considers herself fortunate in that she had a PE specialist teacher at primary school, which led her to wonder: 'Where have they all gone?' Certainly she achieved a high level of sports skills for her age and participated in many school sports competitions. At secondary school, the involvement in sport continued with a particular focus on, what Maggie termed, 'unusual sports' — volleyball and trampolining. The school was renowned for its ability in these sports and Maggie spent most week-ends away at competitions, particularly in volleyball, all over the country. Recounting this led her to make the observation: 'Do you know, now that I'm sitting down talking about it I just think how lucky I've been.' She admires her physical education teachers for the time they gave: 'It's the fact that they loved their job enough I think to want to give up, *numerous, numerous* — not just like a Saturday — we went away for weekends upon weekends.'

Maggie's enthusiasm for sport, and her admiration for her physical education teachers did, eventually, lead her into teacher training. However, she almost took a completely different career path as the result of a disastrous move to an unsuitable sixth form college. She did very well at 'O' level and was encouraged to leave all her 'sports chums' at their school to attend a college with a better reputation. However, Maggie did not adjust well, was lonely and unhappy and lost her enthusiasm for both sport and education. She achieved reasonable 'A' level grades in spite of this, but had no clear direction: 'I went to work in a bank and discovered alcohol, you know, massive amounts of it actually (laughs) and I played netball for the bank and a bit of football but that's it. Jacked in the volleyball entirely — no volleyball at all. And regret it. *Regret it a lot.*' Although Maggie had a good time — 'a great laugh, I was out all the time' — she reached a point two years later where her health was beginning to suffer and she realized that she wanted more from life. She had wanted to teach since childhood: 'like between these two families, I was constantly setting up schools in a little shed. I got them in there and they had no light so they couldn't see but *by God* they were going to learn (laughs).' Maggie deliberated between training for English or physical education, chose physical education on a whim, and embarked upon a new phase in her life.

Teacher training was hugely successful and enjoyable for Maggie: '*I just had the best years of my life*. Best decision I made, ever. *Thank God* that I did it.' She enjoyed student life but, after her previous experiences, was not tempted by the excesses of the social scene: 'everyone was a *party animal* and I was detoxing'. She rediscovered her enthusiasm for sport and threw herself into the academic work: 'I *did* read, I actually *bought books* and read them. Because I wanted to and I didn't care what other people thought.' Maggie enjoyed excellent relationships with academic staff and felt that she was encouraged and supported at every stage of her course — a marked contrast to her experience at sixth form college where she lost all confidence in her ability. The result was a first class honours degree.

After college, Maggie was offered an excellent post in a prestigious school, but had to change her plans as a result of a harrowing family bereavement. Instead, she taught in a small girls' school, which she describes as 'a nice *safe* teaching environment at the time' but, after two years, decided that she was ready for something more challenging. Her current post is as head of girls' physical education in a mixed school.

Maggie thoroughly enjoys her job. As was noted earlier she, rather apologetically, identifies extra-curricular teaching as the high point of teaching:

'this is going to sound really awful, I mean I enjoy my lessons but I love my extra-curricular.' Her apology is based on the assumption that she will sound elitist, but she recounts tales of pupils who have undergone transformations at school as a direct result of their interest and involvement in extra-curricular sport. As a result, Maggie is convinced that this is central to her work as a physical education teacher, even though she is not sure if her view is entirely fashionable:

> I think this business about kids enjoying lessons enough to want to come to clubs after school, to then want to go and do things outside — that's really important to me . . . all kids are welcome regardless, we're not elitist, although we're developing quite strong teams funnily enough — we just happen to be doing that . . . I should be really talking about managing to get a kid with one arm to do something amazing in gymnastics. I should be saying that in *my* lesson the kid with one arm climbed a rope. I can't — I'm not saying that though.

Understandably, given Maggie's philosophy, the low points of teaching centre on pupils' lack of experience as they enter Year 7:

> . . . the frustration at starting from scratch in Year 7 when we should be building on what's happened in primary schools — big frustration that we get kids in with absolutely appalling basic — *basic* — movement skills and I think that has got a very big knock-on effect. I think there's a lot of kids who are in the *under-achieving* bracket for quite a proportion of their school time because so much time is wasted in the early years.

In personal terms, another frustration for Maggie is that not all departmental colleagues are committed to furthering their professional development in physical education, partially because they have so many other roles outside of the department. Thus, she feels that it is difficult to develop the physical education curriculum: 'I'll never be able to do it at [current school], I know that, I'm resigned to the fact that I'm gonna have to leave.' She loves her job and, although she acknowledges that there are monotonous elements to teaching, she finds that the children are constantly changing and that is the key factor: 'everyday something positive happens'.

The future is rather unclear to Maggie at present. She is certain that she wants to build her career in secondary education, but is in need of some advice on career development. Whilst being an enthusiastic supporter of Continuing Professional Development for teachers in schools, she is dismissive of the concept in practice, having seen no evidence of it in either of her two teaching posts. She feels, therefore, that she has no-one with whom she can discuss her needs and her ambitions. She is particularly concerned that 'you can stagnate so easily in teaching' and is striving to keep up to date and to encounter new ideas. Her departmental colleagues are less enthusiastic, however, or at least have a different focus, and Maggie feels rather isolated.

Centrally, the problem is that Maggie is an exceptionally able, analytical individual who needs to be able to share her thoughts with a like-minded colleague. She relishes the opportunity to consider ideas and options — even to the extent that she found our interviews stimulating:

> I'm thinking things out as I'm talking . . . it's weird to be in this situation where I'm actually talking to someone *about what I do* in school, *why* I do it in school . . . initially, I really had to *think* but we don't get that opportunity in school.

If she is to fulfil her ambitions in teaching, it seems likely that Maggie will need to find an outlet for her creative and analytical talents — either in the form of colleagues with whom she can share ideas or by undertaking further educational research. It is clear that she will never be content to stagnate: at the end of our discussion she began to consider the possibilities of conducting research into systems of Continuing Professional Development . . .

Maggie's Comments About Her Story

This was very spooky to read. It is a generally accurate account of our discussions but I sound so poxy at times. My boyfriend really took the mickey out of me! I almost found some of your comments about me uncomfortable to read simply because I'm not used to having someone express a view on me. My initial appraisal was never completed and I've had no feedback on my teaching or my philosophies about PE and education since I left college. This ties in with the issue relating to CPD, or the lack of it, in schools. I am also not very good at accepting 'compliments'. I hate the thought of being regarded as a 'creep' or, as the kids at school call it, a 'boffin'.

Seriously, though, I really wish you luck with the next process. I would have enjoyed reading about PE teachers before I became one and the case-studies offer a sense of realism rather than just speculation. We are often the subject of stereotypes — I just wonder whether we end up fulfilling them!

Believe it or not, my boyfriend was stimulated sufficiently to have a heated debate with me about PE, PE teachers and education, as a result of reading this!

The Final Word

As this book was going to press, Maggie secured a lecturing post in a university. Her main role is in physical education teacher education, and she has been encouraged to pursue her research ideas.

Chapter 9

Grant

Grant is 34 years old and has recently been appointed head of physical education in a mixed grammar school. He is an enthusiastic advocate of physical education and he is keen to promote all forms of sport. His mission is to promote physical education in his school, to provide 'proper' sports coaching for pupils and to encourage all interested staff in the school to become involved with the work of the PE department. He is a successful teacher who intends to pursue his career within the field of physical education/sport, rather than through promotion to senior management level in a secondary school. Since leaving initial teacher training, he has taught in four different schools, has gained an MA (education) from the Open University and is currently in the final stages of an MSc in Sport Sciences.

For Grant, physical education is fundamentally about *doing* and about finding a sport or an activity which will keep pupils active after compulsory schooling:

> As far as I'm concerned, it's for the kids' interest, for the kids who like doing PE, to keep them fit and healthy and to try and get them to enjoy and take part in PE. And if they can find one sport or one activity which they enjoy, and then they can carry on playing it when they leave school and into adulthood and for the rest of their life — then, that's *it* as far as I'm concerned.

Although seeing value in the National Curriculum, Grant has little time for anything which detracts from the practical focus of the subject: 'Getting them thinking about this and evaluating this and doing that — I'm not really interested in that at the moment.' He suggests that this may be because he just doesn't understand enough about it but, fundamentally, he wants the pupils to gain sufficient enjoyment from their physical education lessons to encourage them to become involved in the wide range of extra-curricular activities offered. He is keen to see pupils excel, but 'if they just want to come along and take part and play a bit, that's fine as well'. He is also determined to help pupils master sports techniques 'making sure kids *do the techniques right*', but he is realistic about the limitations he faces: 'So long as we've had a go and tried to teach the pupil — we can only do so much

— if the kid can't play a forehand correctly but they still enjoy playing tennis, they find it fun, then so be it.' Ultimately, Grant measures his success on pupils' activity levels once they have left school: 'If they don't find a sport, then, I suppose in a way we've failed and *I* haven't really achieved what I see as my objective for them.'

Grant is interested in the health and fitness aspect of physical education, particularly in enhancing pupils' understanding of the need to be physically active. He feels that he can have some influence on pupils' fitness levels, although lack of curriculum time is a constant problem. He has found that the best way to teach fitness principles, and to keep children active, is to work through specific sporting activities:

> If you say to the kids — right, we're going to do a bit of fitness work today, they moan, whereas if you do an active lesson, they're probably getting fitter but they don't realize it, I mean, I was the same at school, I didn't enjoy doing training sessions until I got to about 17 or 18.

For Grant, an acceptance that it is impossible to achieve *everything* he would wish, is no reason to stop trying to achieve as much as possible. Although pupils' fitness gains are hard to quantify, he is certain that his work with pupils is having *some* positive impact even though this seems to contradict the received wisdom: 'Perhaps we *think* we're not achieving very much, it's difficult, I suppose we're always reading things, hearing things, like Neil Armstrong, things in the paper about children's fitness levels and you sort of take it in.' In a sense, Grant is determined to battle on, in spite of the many limitations he acknowledges. This philosophy is reflected in his identification of criteria for a successful physical education department. Firstly, he notes the importance of staff working together, based upon experiences in his last post:

> . . . it was a *very difficult school* , the kids were quite a handful and we had a successful department because we all worked together. I think that's important because if you haven't got the staff and they're not prepared to work for each other and work together then you're gonna struggle.

All the other criteria for a successful department relate to pupils: pupils enjoying physical education, improving their skills, gaining some fitness and taking part in sport once they have left school; in summary, 'the best indicator is the kids'. He places a strong emphasis upon the 'fun' element of physical education. For Grant, a measure of a department's success would be that pupils should be disappointed if a PE lesson is cancelled — even if it is only the lesser of two evils. He further feels that one of the fundamental responsibilities of his job is to enable pupils to access the available sporting opportunities — from recreational participation to national representative level, depending on the pupils' abilities. As was noted earlier, an impact upon pupils' fitness is seen as important by Grant: 'But whether we can actually achieve it or not — I don't know. I *think* it's important. Well, I *know* it's important.' Finally, involvement in sport once pupils have left school is the ultimate test of a department's success.

It is unsurprising, perhaps, that Grant sees physical education and sport as, at the very least, closely related. Although he has analysed the sport/ physical education relationship at a theoretical level in both Masters degree courses, he remains unconvinced that there is any difference between the two:

> I've never really known the difference . . . I can't see it because we do a load of sports in physical education . . . in the National Curriculum document it says physical education is this, this and this. 'Raising the Game' says sport is this, this and this and you sort of look at it and you say — well, it's basically the same thing.

Furthermore, Grant is unconvinced that the National Curriculum has offered any new insights: 'it's basically what we would do anyway but you've just got to write it down on paper — formalise it — and waste a lot of time . . . I think it's pretty sick'. At a practical level, however, he can see that the National Curriculum has altered the way the curriculum is designed and managed, and he can certainly see the value of written guidelines for the subject. Where he has a problem is when the policies become over-bearing. Thus, anything which detracts from his personal mission to get pupils involved in *doing* practical sport is, for Grant, merely an irritation.

Although Grant has taught in four schools, it is only in his current school that he has found a supportive and interested senior management team. At his interview, the school philosophy was discussed and he was invited to analyse the match between that philosophy and his own views. Management enthusiasm for physical education was evident right from the interview stage. In previous schools, he concluded that he has never really known what senior managers wanted, or what they thought of the subject or his work except, perhaps, on one occasion in his last post when a new headteacher expressed a concern about sports day. She felt that a 'fun' approach should be taken — as Grant put it: 'bean bags in a bucket and little races'. Grant was horrified: 'I said to her — well I said it a bit more politely — well you may have done that in your old school but we're not childminding, not here to play fun and games . . . that's not what we're about, you know, we want to actually do something properly.' Such differences in opinion contributed to Grant's decision to change jobs.

Similarly, it is only in his new post in the grammar school that Grant has experienced supportive and enthusiastic colleagues from other departments who are willing to help with practices and fixtures: 'It's been chalk and cheese — I've gone from one extreme to the other.' In his previous school, 13 of the 80 staff (including PE staff) expressed some interest in helping out, but there were perennial problems once the initial enthusiasm had dwindled: 'You'd get cold weather and they wouldn't want to go outside and they'd come down at lunchtime in their clothes and they'd be 20 minutes late.' In the end, the problems outweighed the advantages and many of the clubs had to be cancelled. In contrast, Grant now has the avid support of almost half of the staff, to the extent that individuals have volunteered help without being asked: 'I used to run a football team last year, is it all right if I do it again?' Once he had recovered from the shock, Grant was delighted and he now enjoys the extra scope which such support offers. In speculating upon the reasons for the differences between the two schools, tradition and a respect for sport seem to be the central issues:

> I think *partly* the reason is because we're a grammar school and whether it's those old traditional values — that sport is probably more valued in a grammar school — I don't know, but it's the idea you get that sport was a very big part of a grammar school education and a lot of the staff have been there for a long time.

Interestingly, Grant has also met two of the governors at his current school and both have expressed interest in physical education and have offered support: 'whereas I never had that in my last school, in fact the governors could have walked around the school and I wouldn't have known who they were'. It is, perhaps, easy to see why Grant is enjoying his new job. He appears to have found a niche which enables him, even encourages him, to pursue his vision of a practical, sporting physical education.

Grant's passion for sport stems from an active childhood where sport was central. Although his parents were not 'sporty', his grandfather was something of a family sporting hero 'and I assume that must be where I picked it up from'. Grant played a whole range of sports at primary school — including extra-curricular practices in cricket and football. He also made friends on the basis of sporting interests:

> I always ended up being friends with them and so I assume we used to play a lot of sports together and then the other children who lived in the street — we used to have an alley out the back — and I can remember playing tennis. We used to get some deckchairs and use them as nets and draw lines in chalk for the court, and playing cricket in the back alley and

football in the road — I remember all those types of things. It was just what young boys did.

Grant remembers no specific teaching or coaching from these early days, but lots of playing. Similarly, at secondary school, although he was involved in football and cricket, and represented the school in both sports, he remembers little skills teaching:

> No, it was just a case of, you know, 'there's a ball fellas now go and play and if you need me I'm in my office' . . . I never remember getting any coaching. No-one ever said to me 'do this, do that, try and do this, try and do that' either at football, rugby, tennis — *any sport*. The first time I ever got coached was when I went to college.

Although Grant is glad that he had so many sporting opportunities 'football matches every Saturday morning, football every Wednesday afternoon, so we were playing twice a week, cricket matches, rugby matches' he regrets that he had so little skills teaching: 'Now that I think back to it I really feel a bit angry and frustrated because I feel had I ever got taught or coached when I was bit younger, I might have been better at something.' He values the time his physical education teachers gave to fixtures, but feels that his sporting career has suffered from a lack of coaching. It would appear that Grant learnt everything from watching other people and from participating. He even reached county football level, without ever having been taught or coached. He was disappointed to find that at county training, he still encountered little skills teaching. Fundamentally, he succeeded to the level he did because 'all I ever wanted to do was play sport'.

As with other teachers in this study, Grant's physical education teacher was a key influence on his decision to enter teacher training. Grant selected the same training college as his teacher and enjoyed every moment of the college experience:

> . . . it was so much freedom, you make your own decisions, whatever you decide you can do, got to be responsible for everything you do. *It was good* because we were doing sport pretty much *all day every day* which was really what I *absolutely loved*, you know.

Importantly, Grant encountered some 'real' coaching and teaching at last, and he thoroughly appreciated it: 'you start to get a better understanding and you improve your *own* game'.

Although Grant chose the four-year dedicated BEd route at college, he has since decided that a more general Sport Sciences degree, followed by a one year postgraduate qualification, would have been a better choice. His reasons for this centre on his consuming interest in sport:

> I think, having done the education and gone into teaching, all I've ever known is the *school* side of it, the *education* side of it, you know . . . I just think if I was doing a BSc I'd learn more about *sport* as well . . . and what I'm doing now, with my MSc [in sport sciences] and my 'A' level teaching is I'm going into the theory side of it because that's really now what I'm finding a bit more interesting rather than just education, education, education.

Grant has come to the view that much of the education theory he learnt at college was placed too early in his career — and, furthermore, that most of it could more usefully have been 'picked up' in the course of teaching, where it would have had more meaning. He therefore places little value on the education courses that he attended at college, in fact he can't remember much about them. He remembers most of his practical physical education courses, however, and he values them greatly. He now feels that he needs to gain more specific subject knowledge if he is to help pupils to achieve the goals of physical education as he had identified them.

Still a keen sportsman, Grant finds that much of his time is now spent on school sporting commitments. He thoroughly enjoys this and, unsurprisingly, sees the development of pupils' sporting skills as one of the 'highs' of teaching:

> . . . the good things are, basically, it's having a good lesson — when you've taught a lesson and the kids have worked well and actually, sometimes you can see a definite progression, a definite development of skills over the course of only one hour . . . and then over the course of five or six weeks, if things have gone really well, that, for me, has been the high point of teaching . . . I wouldn't say my career has actually *had* any highs in terms of anything else.

Becoming a head of department is not really viewed as a 'high' by Grant. He is, however, delighted with the attainment of his Full Badge, one of the most prestigious coaching awards in football, more particularly because he hadn't encountered coaching in any form until college: '*that was a real high*'. He also feels proud that he recently won his golf club scratch championship and that he has reached county standard in golf — all the more so because he only started playing eight years ago. He was pleased with the award of his first Masters degree, but that was in education and he is now more interested in his work in sport sciences. He is certain that achieving the MSc in Sport Sciences will be a high point.

The lows for Grant centre on a lack of support for physical education which he found in previous teaching posts: 'The real lows have just been the battles you fight against senior management within schools trying to get any kind of *fair play* towards physical education.' His passion for sport and for physical education cannot tolerate schools where there is a lack of respect for his subject. He takes the lack of enthusiasm personally. As he notes: 'If you've got senior managers who actually value PE and see it as important, it makes a *hell of a difference,* well certainly to me as a teacher and what I'm actually doing and my *enthusiasm* and my general commitment to the job.'

It is clear that the future for Grant will be in jobs which can accommodate his passion for his subject and will value his goals for pupils in sport. He will search for options where he perceives there is 'fair play' for physical education and he is considering lecturing in higher education as an option. Whilst in schools, it is clear that Grant will continue to strive to provide high quality teaching and coaching, ensuring that pupils do not suffer from a lack of coaching in the way that he suffered. He is professional, committed and driven to do his best to ensure that pupils can enjoy and succeed in sport.

Grant's Comments About His Story

I suppose it does sound like me, although some of the things I say do have high levels of cringe value. It's almost like I'm at a job interview. My comments sound very idealistic and some just downright blase. On the whole, I think this sums up my views and feelings about PE, especially the comment in the last two sentences. I have recognized this as my 'driving force' for a number of years now.

The Final Word

Grant has since applied for posts in higher education, and has decided to continue with research by registering for a doctorate.

Part Three

The Theme Chapters

Chapter 10

Physical Education and Sport: Conflict or Continuum?

Introduction

The relationship between physical education and sport is both simple and complex. In one sense, it couldn't be more straightforward. Physical education teachers teach pupils, in schools, how to play and understand a range of sports and physical activities. Historically, and now enshrined within the National Curriculum, that includes dance. Add to that the facts that many physical education teachers are, or have been, notable sports participants, and that some are also sports coaches in their spare time (Chelladurai and Kuga, 1996), and the physical education/sport relationship would appear to be clear — even cosy. However, teachers in this book have expressed a more complex understanding of their roles. Many of them have sought to place a distance between physical education and sport, and their views are well supported by the physical education literature. As Sage (1996) notes, 'Although sports are typically one component of a physical education curriculum, current literature in both physical education and sport typically goes to great lengths to conceptually differentiate the two' (p. 452). Yet, although statements about the distance between physical education and sport are made with firm conviction, the explanations for those convictions seem rather less certain. It could even be argued that for some in the profession, belief in the separation of physical education and sport has almost taken on the characteristics of a faith — difficult to explain, so deemed to be beyond question or logical reason.

The purpose of this chapter is to try to understand more about the nature of the relationship between sport and physical education, particularly where they meet in the context of secondary education. To this end, evidence from the case-study teachers provides a starting point for the discussion. Their comments point to a need for further consideration of several key — although not new — issues: an analysis of language used in education and physical education; a discussion on the possible reasons for seeking to distinguish between physical education and sport; an analysis of underlying philosophical issues about perceptions of 'mind', 'body', and different 'types'

of knowledge in education and physical education; and, finally, to conclusions about the relationship between education, physical education and
sport. In many ways, this chapter represents a personal voyage of understanding for us, the authors. In reflecting on our own practice as teachers
and lecturers, we felt that distinctions between physical education and sport
were conceptually unclear. At the same time, such distinctions were clearly
very important to several of the teachers we interviewed. In short, this
chapter can be described as a test of faith.

What the Teachers Said

In summary, six of the eight case-study teachers felt it was important to
make a distinction between physical education and sport. Jane raised the
issue in our earliest interview. She made a distinction between education
(learning), and sport (doing/participating):

> Well there's a link between the two, but, I think when we're talking about
> physical education we're really talking about education — acquisition of
> knowledge, understanding and . . . give them the feel behind something
> and not *necessarily* that they can do it but at least that they know about
> their bodies and they've got a clear understanding of how to get fit even if
> they're not. But sport is just *doing* it.

Arnold saw physical education in broad, holistic terms; sport was something far more narrow. Essentially, he wanted to teach pupils the rudiments
of sports skills and understanding, such that they could be informed participants and spectators. He hoped that his teaching method was 'educational'
in that he helped pupils to interact and to care for others:

> I think for most of our courses, we are attempting to give them an idea of
> the skills involved in various sports, and our club facilities and our team
> games should be complementing that for the ones that actually want to
> improve or go further and need coaching . . . And I also try to use the
> reciprocal method of working, of helping each other and, er, everyone
> trying to spot each other's mistakes, that sort of thing — to improve their
> skills and to improve their relationships with others in the group, uhm, to
> be supportive of those who find it difficult, and I also think it does im-
> prove skills as well.

Diane's views were similar to Jane's, although she gave rather more detail
in her rationale. However, she began to contradict herself as her explanation
progressed:

> I think there is a definite difference in that we [in physical education] are teaching them how to do the activities, and they are learning about their bodies, and how to use their minds as well, and all the social and emotional things that come into it. Whereas sport, I always see as out of school, they're just doing things — doing the activity, and so education is them learning about themselves and the activity, whereas sport — they're just doing it. I mean they do coincide in school, where they actually get into a game at the end and they actually do the activity — and, I suppose, in clubs. They are mutually beneficial, yes. The education side is obviously more intense, but then you learn anyway when you play sport — like to interact with other people and taking responsibility in, for example, a team.

On the other hand, Laura was very clear about her aims from the outset: 'I see my role and the role of my subject as to enhance their [pupils'] self-esteem' and that included making a clear distinction between a teacher and a sports coach:

> If you get some one in that's purely football focused or purely basketball focused, then they're purely focused on their sport. They are focused on being the best lay-up merchant, the best free-throw merchant, whatever . . . whereas when I'm educating, I'm not isolating one or certain members of the groups, as I'm educating to a whole range of pupils and so that all pupils will achieve.

Edgar had a similar philosophy, in that he stressed the importance of *education*. Furthermore, he saw physical education as the natural home for those pupils who are struggling academically and socially:

> PE itself though has its own importance, in that it gives the less academic kids a chance to shine at something. I think PE can also raise the confidence of kids, especially those who aren't really academic, and not respected in any other subject. Yeah . . . it's definitely an area for self-expression and to develop feelings of self-worth and self-confidence.

Thus he suggested that physical education should strive to be:

> Something that's interesting, challenging, creative and progressive. The kids should be pushed individually, so there should be a system of individual differentiation between the kids. We should really try to incorporate the social aspect a lot more in that we, and the subject, should help kids understand that they need others to get on in life.

Maggie was certain that physical education and sport should be differentiated, but was having increasing difficulty making sense of her own views in the context of the pressing needs of practice:

> I used to think I was going to change the world and it's gone full cycle and I feel now that I want more and more to concentrate on achieving the basics.

She suggested that 'we are *teaching sport*, but we're using [sport] as a vehicle to open up a lot of other avenues', and then she gave the following explanation:

> . . . there are some general principles in netball that apply in other sports, so you'd use catching and throwing and shooting which then apply in basket-ball. There are things that apply in netball, basketball, that then apply in all sports — etiquette, safety, health. But then you expand it even further and it then becomes (long pause) a social attitude that by relating to people in a sporting context, you learn how to relate to people in life, in general.

As was noted in Chapter 8, this discussion led to Maggie attempting a reappraisal of the whole concept of physical education — including the title, which she ended up changing to 'physical, sport and health education'.

In contrast, the other two teachers in the study saw little difference between physical education and sport; on the contrary, the concepts were viewed as compatible, or even one and the same thing. For Pete, physical education is, quite simply, the means to nurture pupils' talents in sport. Thus, he strives for:

> Successful teams, successful individuals in individual sports. I firmly be-lieve that this brings — it sets standards and it raises the less able to be better than less able. In comparison they'll always be less able than the top ones within the group but I think the overall standard will raise. Standards were far higher at this school when we pushed for more excellence.

Finally, as was noted in the introduction to this book, and in his story, Grant admitted 'I've never really known the difference . . . I can't see it because we do a load of sports in physical education'. Furthermore, he pointed out that, in his view, and despite claims to the contrary in both the National Curriculum for Physical Education (see DES, 1992) and *Sport, Raising the Game* (see DNH, 1995) 'you sort of look at it and you say — well, it's basically the same thing'.

So, where do the teachers' comments lead us? A flippant answer would be 'everywhere and nowhere!' Taken together, perhaps the most signific-ant feature about these comments is their individuality. They certainly make it difficult to determine what the nature of the relationship between phys-ical education and sport is, or should be except, perhaps, to confirm that it is contested. Clearly, more evidence is required to make progress on this question.

Language

Maggie's idea for a change of title from 'physical education' to 'physical, sport and health education' is a useful starting point for this investigation. Her suggestion was based upon a belief that the title of the subject doesn't adequately reflect its content or purpose. But does it matter — or is this just an exercise in semantics?

Pring (1976, p. 15) highlighted the dynamic nature of language, in that it:

> ... offers richness and complexity. It gives the individual not only a detached understanding of the world but some purpose on it, and a capacity to bend it to his (sic) purposes.

Furthermore, Hirst (1974) notes that language is central in the development of understanding and, if this is accepted, then the title 'physical education' deserves some scrutiny. Certainly, numerous authors have pointed to the problems of definition which bedevil physical education (Macdonald and Brooker, 1997; Tinning, Kirk, Evans and Glover, 1994; Stroot, 1994) and Kirk (1994) suggests that this makes it impossible to have a clear understanding of the physically educated pupil. It is unsurprising, therefore, that there is a lack of clarity in the nature of the relationship between physical education, sport and education. Furthermore, research confirms that this is not just a local, or even a national issue, but an international question. In Australia, Brooker and Macdonald (1995) chart the problems that physical education faces in establishing its identity in the context of competing discourses of health, sport, academic study and science. They conclude: 'Consequently, PE knowledge has been conceptualised and practised in many forms, serving many masters' (p. 108). Similarly, in America, Seidentop (1987) suggests that physical education has lost sight of its purposes, with goals which are too 'fuzzy' to be meaningful. As a result, he has advocated 'Sport Education' as a clearer way forward for schools and pupils. Evans (1990) agrees that the current position is confusing and unhelpful, and reports that in his experience in Australia, it would be almost impossible to distinguish between what is understood as 'sport' in schools and what is taught under the label 'physical education'. More recently in Australia and New Zealand, programmes such as Aussie Sport and Kiwisport have been introduced — ostensibly to supplement, rather than replace, existing physical education. The impact of these initiatives has been such that they enjoy a much higher media profile, because of their clear association with sport, than the traditional physical education programme (Thorpe, 1996).

England, attempts were made during the formulation of the National
lum for Physical Education to make a working distinction between
sport:

1.1   In *physical education* the emphasis is on learning in a mainly physical
       context. The purpose of the learning is to develop specific knowledge,
       skills and understanding and to promote physical development and
       competence. The learning promotes participation in sport.

1.2   *Sport* is the term applied to a range of physical activities where
       emphasis is on participation and competition. Different sporting act-
       ivities can and do contribute to learning. (DES, 1992)

This was the result of a lengthy attempt to achieve clarity, by a working
group of committed individuals at all levels of the PE profession. And yet
the outcome was, arguably, both circular and confusing. Perhaps there is a
prior question here which has been missed: What could be the purpose of
making the distinction at all?

Why Seek to Make a Distinction Between Physical Education and Sport?

The answer is, probably, status. Sport, in an academic framework, has little
status, and so the physical education profession has sought to describe and
justify its activities in ways which are deemed to be educationally superior.
Yet, physical education continues to be a low-status subject in schools — a
fact which is almost undisputed in the literature. For example, Evans, Penney
and Davies (1996) note: 'Historically, PE has struggled for recognition and
status as a subject within the curriculum of state schools' (p. 5; also, see next
chapter). It would appear then, that in the bid for recognition and status,
physical education teachers have sought to present themselves as much 'more'
than teachers of sport. Instead, they have justified their existence by drawing
upon what they perceive are more 'valued' claims for their role (Beck, 1990;
Talbot 1987; Reid, 1996a). The teachers in this book are no exception —
and yet the strategy seems to have failed (Macdonald and Brooker, 1997).
Indeed, status is a concern so central to the lives and careers of physical
education teachers that it is explored as a discrete issue in Chapter 11, but it
also emerges as significant in all the theme chapters.
    Thorpe (1996) suggests that 'conflicts about sport and PE only arise
when people are ill-informed and/or insecure' (p. 155) and he cites a number
of examples in Britain which demonstrate how the worlds of physical education and sport can work together for the benefit of pupils. For example:

... the British Council of Physical Education (BCPE), National Coaching Foundation and Sports Council liaison with National Governing Bodies, which led, with the support of two experienced physical educators respected in the sports world, to a resource for primary schools. (cited in Read and Edwards, 1992, p. 146)

Interestingly, few joint initiatives have been started by the physical education profession, and most were received by them — initially at least — with some reservations. As Thorpe puts it, physical educators tend to 'look with suspicion and, perhaps, a little envy at the growth of the sporting lobby' (1996, p. 146). In Thorpe's terms then, the physical education profession could be described as 'insecure'. Kirk and Tinning (1990) are rather more scathing: they suggest that physical educators have been 'more concerned with following trends, with showing that we can fit whatever role society requires of us' (p. 2). At this point, the discussion seems to become circular. As Macdonald and Brooker (1997) argue: 'an outcome of definitional problems for physical education has been a lack of clarity, purpose and parameters for success in physical education programs' (p. 157) and perhaps we need to revisit Maggie's dilemma about the title 'physical education' to further the analysis.

A Return to Language

'Physical education' as a subject title, may have two unhelpful characteristics. The first is that of breadth. 'Physical education' is as broad, and as vague, as would be the logically comparable term 'mind education'. Such a comparison suggests that physical education may be trying to do too much, or that it has failed to identify a specific focus within its huge potential. If this is the case, then a clear delineation of the discrete activities of physical education could be a useful step towards finding that focus, and it could be argued that this is one of the key achievements of the National Curriculum. Indeed this underpins Thorpe's (1996) belief that 'There has never been a better time to resolve issues of sport within the PE curriculum' (p. 155). However, such a content-led approach to understanding the curriculum is not new. Pring, in 1976, rejected reductionist views of knowledge and urged analysts instead to recognize the diversity and value of activities already in the curriculum. In this spirit, Meakin (1983) noted that

Physical education, in its present form, is devoid of any strict logical unity, by which I mean that there is no feature, or set of features, both common and peculiar to all the activities currently falling under its name. (p. 11)

85

Meakin followed this line of thinking to present, what was at the time, a very stark account of the nature and purpose of physical education:

> By physical education, I shall mean the attempt to educate pupils (or at least contribute to their education) by seriously engaging them in the following kinds of activity;
> 1. competitive games and athletic events, plus those physical activities which, while not competitive in themselves, are practised in a competitive way
> 2. educational and formal gymnastics
> 3. dance and dance-like activities
> 4. non-competitive outdoor pursuits
> 5. swimming. (pp. 10–11)

Today, Meakin's analysis looks remarkably like an advance copy of the National Curriculum! More recently, Reid (1996a) endorsed Meakin's position by agreeing that physical education lacks a unifying 'essence', arguing: 'it is, simply the name which we give to the diverse activities of the physical education curriculum' (p. 11). Thus, Reid overcomes the breadth and the lack of focus that are implied by the term 'physical education' by stating simply that 'physical education . . . is to be defined as "what physical educators do"' (p. 10). Earlier, Keddie (1971) offered essentially the same analysis of all curriculum areas: 'subjects are what practitioners do with them' (p. 44).

Some of the teachers in this book would probably agree. Maggie, for example, suggested that the legal framework of the National Curriculum for Physical Education has had relatively little impact upon teachers' practice. On the other hand, Arnold might dispute the implication that he has so much freedom.

A second difficulty with the term 'physical education' is its unavoidable suggestion of dualism, reinforcing just that Cartesian approach to education that has long bedeviled physical education. In the Cartesian approach, mind and body are seen as separate and, in traditional terms, the education of the mind is viewed as the superior purpose. As Reid (1996a) points out '"physical" seems to speak of the human body, its nature and functioning'. On the other hand, '"education" typically connotes the mind and its development' (p. 8). The outcome of this analysis leads Reid to conclude:

> Physical education, then, gets off to an unpromising start, at the point of baptism indeed, in what looks like an awkward and doomed attempt to reconcile the dualism of mind and body . . . it might even be argued that the very concept involves a logical contradiction. (p. 8)

Furthermore, it is interesting to note that the term 'physical education' was queried on these same grounds, in educational documentation over 40 years ago:

> We are increasingly aware of the wholeness and of the interdependence of those processes that we have been accustomed to describe as physiological and psychological. It may not be long before we realise that the term 'physical' in relation to humanity has a very limited meaning. (Department of Education and Science, 1952, p. 51)

However, Cartesian dualism holds a persistent popular attraction, despite the fact that 'the Cartesian framework has come to be regarded within modern philosophy as fundamentally incoherent' (Reid, 1996a, p. 14). The result of this is that physical educationists have sought ways to link themselves to the mind, or at least to distance themselves from the purely physical, in an attempt to achieve the higher status that they crave. It is surely at this point, at the very heart of the conflict between mind and body, that claims are made for a distinction between physical education and sport. For example, Tinning et al. (1994) argue that physical education must seek its justification in the context of education, rather than emphasize its links with sport. But there's the rub. Physical education, in its manifestation on the school curriculum *is indeed the teaching of sport*, or at least it often looks very much like it. Timetable headings such as 'Year 7 netball' and 'Year 10 football' would seem to indicate that sport is taking place. Furthermore, the physical education teacher visibly spends much time teaching pupils within the framework of specific sports, including sport-specific rules, equipment and pitches. It could be argued that in seeking to justify itself in almost ethereal terms, physical education simply reinforces the notion that practical work is of low status — yet it is likely to remain an essentially practical subject! Indeed, the teachers in this book identified teaching practical activities, and particularly sports and sports skills, as the high point of teaching (see Chapter 13).

Peters (1966) stated that subjects should be justified on their own worth and, similarly, Arnold (1985) has long cautioned against justifying physical education by reference to, what he terms, its 'spin-offs' or 'beneficial outcomes'. In this context, Arnold (1996) makes a distinction between education and schooling, pointing out that sport is educative when it is 'pursued, in a moral way, for its own internal goals, for its inherent skills, tactics, strategies and standards' (p. 96). On the other hand, when sport is used for other ends 'as a means to promote such external goals as health and fitness, socialization or part of a policy to deter delinquent behaviour, it can be regarded as a form of schooling and not as education' (p. 97). Interestingly, the teachers in this book have identified all of Arnold's 'schooling' examples as central to their understanding of the purpose of physical education: for example, Jane wants pupils to see that they have 'fitness for life'; Diane refers to the importance of 'all the social and emotional things' that are part of physical education; Laura stresses the central requirement to 'enhance (pupils') esteem'; and Edgar thinks that physical education provides an opportunity for less academic pupils 'to shine at something'. In Arnold's (1985) terms, they are stressing the importance of the 'spin-offs', rather than focusing upon the inherent value of the activity itself: thus physical education is reduced to a form of 'schooling' and does not achieve the distinction of being 'education'. This may go some way towards explaining the difficulties physical education teachers face in justifying their subject to the wider educational community, and even to themselves. It could even be suggested that by trying to create a role for themselves which stresses unproven links to the higher status 'mind' activities, or alternatively by distancing themselves from mainly practical purposes, physical education teachers are simply trying to take a short-cut to status (see Chapter 12). In this way, they can avoid difficult questions about the educative nature of practical sports activities by rendering such questions irrelevant. So, is it possible to make a case for the inherent value of practical activities in an educational context, without separating physical education and sport?

Knowing That, Knowing How and 'Just' Doing Sport

Further to the earlier discussion about Cartesian dualism, and the separation of body and mind, Pears (1971) notes the significance of the classic division of knowledge into three 'species': knowledge of facts, acquaintance and knowledge how to do things. In the context of education, a number of influential theorists (Phenix, 1964; Peters, 1966; White, 1973; Hirst, 1974) pointed to the importance of 'knowing that' or, in Hirst's terms, 'propositional knowledge'. Thus, education came to be viewed as an essentially academic enterprise which is linked to the mind (Reid, 1996a), and physical education encountered a problem: it is all too clearly linked to 'know how', practical knowledge, and the body. Popular belief in a split between mind and body seems to endure, yet at the academic level, the theory has been largely discounted (Reid, 1996a). Furthermore, it could be argued that a return to the work of some of the leading proponents of a mind/body split in education — for example, Pring and Hirst — shows that they have been misrepresented, over the years, in several crucial respects.

Ryle (1949) was an early critic of Cartesian dualism, and he attempted to give a more positive account of 'know how': 'We learn *how* by practice, schooled indeed by criticism and example, but often quite unaided by any lesson in the theory' (p. 41). Ryle also makes a case for the learning which is central to 'know how':

> It is of the essence of merely habitual practices that one performance is a replica of its predecessors. It is of the essence of intelligent practices that one performance is modified by its predecessors. The agent is still learning. (p. 42)

At first glance, Pring (1976) would appear to be in conflict with Ryle, thus a poor advocate for a practical subject, when he describes education as: 'the development of such mental qualities which contribute to the life of the mind' (p. 8). But Pring advocates that a 'sufficiently generous analysis of knowledge is accepted' (p. 9) in education, and he argues that we tend to ignore the value of 'know how' only because 'know that' is easier to examine. His case for the importance of 'know how' could be supported by most physical educationists:

> To learn *how* to do something is an achievement that involves an adequate conceptualisation of the problem, certainly, but also coming up to scratch in one's *performance*. (p. 18)

Pring seems to infer that performance in practical activities places greater demands upon an individual than curriculum activities which simply demand 'know that' — a 'more than' approach to physical education which is rather different to that suggested by teachers in this book and other research. For example, both Jane and Diane dismissed pupils' performance in sport as 'just doing it'.

  Hirst (1974) is another unlikely advocate for physical education stressing, as he does, the primacy of cognitive development in education, and the comparatively lower value of practical activities. However, there is some contradiction in Hirst's argument on this issue. For example, he notes that practical performance makes extensive demands upon pupils because it 'always involves knowledge of the first two kinds, but it clearly picks out certain capacities over and above cognitive understanding and mastery' (p. 57). His case rests, therefore, upon the view that the demands of practical activities are inappropriate — because they are beyond the scope of education. Again, the inference seems to be that success in practical activities requires 'more' from pupils than success in other academic activities. Pring (1976) takes the discussion further in his criticism of Hirst's narrow interpretation of appropriate knowledge in education:

Important though it is to know *that* certain statements are true, knowing *how* to do things (to play a piece of music, to enjoy a concert, to make a sketch, to appreciate a poem, to climb skilfully) is equally a cognitive achievement, a development of the mind, which is not reducible to 'knowing that' or to the kinds of knowledge that can be stated in propositions'. (p. 39)

Within physical education, Carr (1983) considers that sports and games must be seen as important in education because they are 'expressions of important human aims, purposes and interests of a social, cultural and individual nature' (p. 8). Meakin (1983) points to the worthwhile knowledge, 'chiefly practical', that can be developed in physical education and he suggests that education would be unsatisfactory without it. Similarly, Reddiford (1983) suggests, simply, 'that physical activities are important to and for our *lives,* when a part of our lives is the history of our bodily activities' (p. 20). Kirk (1988), on the other hand, makes a slightly different claim:

It is important to point out . . . that physical activity does not *lead* to cognitive development, but rather it demands conceptual awareness, knowledge and understanding as a necessary (though not sufficient) part of successful engagement and participation. (p. 79)

But Kirk's position surely leads to a question: if physical activity does draw upon cognitive skills as described, then why preclude the notion of the *development* of those cognitive skills as a result? Could we, as physical educationists, be so bold? And if so, wouldn't this be a rather different approach to that which justifies physical education primarily on other grounds such as moral and social development? Perhaps physical educationists are, indeed, at the heart of the academic enterprise, rather than on its periphery. Perhaps our curriculum activities are important *because* they are 'just sport' rather than in spite of it. Although this would challenge existing educational knowledge hierarchies, a challenge which would undoubtedly meet resistance (Fernandez Balboa, 1995) is this a reason to avoid the battle?

Recently, Reid (1996a,1996b) has conducted a detailed analysis of a range of arguments about physical education, education, and both practical and theoretical knowledge, in the light of Scottish Office Education Department documents about the physical education curriculum. Three of his conclusions are particularly relevant to this discussion:

The new orthodoxy which seeks to redefine physical education in terms of the opportunities which it provides for theoretical study is based on a series of errors. (1996b, p. 102)

The traditional physical education activities of games, gymnastics, dance ؟ so on essentially involve (and the point can scarce be over-emphasized) the exercise of forms of practical knowledge: the idea that their educational significance depends on their being exploited for theoretical purposes of analysis and investigation is the crucial error on which current official policy is based. (1996a, p. 15)

Very little of what I say, however, can lay any claim to originality; and this makes the persistence of what I would regard as mistaken views all the more remarkable, since the instruments for exposing their weaknesses and confusions have been available to theorists of physical education for many years. (1996b, p. 95)

Taking Reid's first two conclusions, analysis in this chapter seems to suggest a prior question: 'Why bother to justify physical education in the manner described?' Perhaps practical activities are valuable for pupils just as they are — including, as is being tentatively argued here, the use and development of much-prized cognitive skills. Perhaps they are the most complete method of education, truly addressing the needs of the whole child.

Reid's (1996b) final charge, if substantiated, is worrying. If the potential exists to ease the relationship between education, physical education and sport by providing evidence of the educational value of our practical activities, then that is what we should do — provide firm research evidence. Instead, and in good faith, theorists have sought to help practitioners by offering them justifications for their subject which stress 'spin-offs' and de-emphasize the very heart of the role of the physical education teacher.

Sport has been shunned as — probably — just too visibly practical, and too closely linked to the highly competitive, slightly distasteful world of professional sport. Yet it is possible to conceive of a school sport ethos which transcends the adult professional version (we would claim that it has existed in schools for years). Perhaps then, we could abandon the somewhat dubious claim that although physical education teachers take their pupils out to the netball court, use netballs, teach netball skills and rules and ultimately how to play the game of netball, they are *really* involved in pupils' health/fitness or social/moral development. Currently, teachers may be concerned that 'simply' teaching pupils sports skills would be viewed as too close to 'mere' coaching — an even lower grade activity, in an educational framework, than teaching physical education. This may explain Laura's comments about the distinction between herself, as a teacher, and the role of a coach. However, physical education teachers might be shocked to hear that there are those in the newly emerging coaching profession who would argue the reverse — that it is coaches who have the more worthwhile, professional role as it is they who have the opportunity to 'teach' most effectively (Chelladurai and Kuga, 1996). If the argument is persuasive, one wonders where that leaves physical education teachers?

Physical Education and Sport: Conflict or Continuum?

At the start of this chapter, it was suggested that belief in the importance of making a firm distinction between physical education and sport had become like a 'faith' for many in the physical education profession. Thus, it is a belief which few are able to challenge, especially as sport appears to have such low status on educational measures. Yet, physical education teachers are visibly and inextricably associated with sport, both in their jobs and in other spheres of their lives (Armour, 1997). Arguments to the contrary appear to be lost on many colleagues, parents and pupils.

To summarize, the reasons for seeking to make a distinction between physical education and sport may be understandable. However, none of the resulting justifications for physical education, such as those exemplified by teachers in this book, has made any impact upon the low status of the subject in schools. Teachers use the arguments which they are taught in their training, and which are expected by their senior managers — all to little effect. One can only wonder at the perseverance of physical education teachers. Clearly then, the issue of status needs further exploration, and this is the focus of the next chapter. The final point to be made in this chapter is a positive one. Perhaps there is another way to justify physical education in an educational context — and maybe it lies in returning to some of the central daily activities of physical education teachers: teaching identifiable sports, physical activities, dance and practical skills — and, through research, seeking to understand more about their educational value for pupils. Thus sport and physical education, at the school level, would become one. And if we follow Pring's (1976) lead, perhaps we can begin to show that our subject demands *more* of pupils than other curriculum areas — education of the 'whole child' in the most literal sense. This, of course, would include cognitive development, but only as one part of the multitude of educational outcomes which we may be able to claim. But do we have the courage — or will faith blind us?

Chapter 11

Striving for Status in the Education Club: 'Us', 'Them' and 'We'

Introduction

Establishing status and credibility in an educational framework has long been an elusive goal for the physical education profession. Status implies respect, and respect confers credibility and value upon a subject and its teachers. From the vantage point of the physical education teacher, such status resides, primarily, in the more traditional academic curriculum areas (Reid, 1997). The teachers in this book confirmed that physical education is indeed a low-status subject, and their views are well supported by international research, both current and historical (Morgan, 1974; Paul, 1996; Moreira, Sparkes and Fox, 1995; Stroot et al., 1994; Sparkes, Templin and Schempp, 1990). However, many of the teachers' stories were also evidence of an astonishing resilience in the face of indifference about physical education from colleagues and managers in schools. Central to this was the view that, individually, physical education teachers could (and should) challenge preconceptions about physical education — either through setting an example, personally, of a committed and intelligent professional, or through visible and popular curriculum innovation. So, although the teachers accepted that their subject had low status, most of them were not *resigned* to it, rather they were battling against it. The difficulty with this position is, however, that it leaves teachers with the daily burden of trying to prove themselves. Unsurprisingly, an element of weariness was evident in some of the teachers' stories, and this is an issue which arises again in the final chapter on teachers' careers.

This chapter investigates the status issue in three main areas. As in the last chapter, the teachers' comments from the case-study stories are the starting point for the discussion. Even taken alone, they tell a sorry tale about status and physical education. Following those comments, further investigation of the issue leads to analysis, firstly, of the role of the physical education profession ('Us') in creating its own difficulties. This includes an examination of the value of two explicit 'status-solutions' offered by the case-study teachers: health/fitness and examinations. Secondly, the role of the broader education community ('Them') in sustaining those difficulties is investigated. Finally, the potential for cooperation within the teaching profession ('We') is considered, and a case is made for research which helps physical education teachers to justify the largest and, arguably, most visible part of their job: teaching practical activities. Although teachers in this book also claimed that physical education is an important vehicle for social and moral education, this arose in the broader context of complex perceptions about their 'caring' roles as teachers, and it forms the central theme of the next chapter.

'Us' and 'Them' in the Teachers' Stories

In many cases, the stories teachers told made it clear that low professional status was an accepted part of their lives. Thus, they tended to raise the issue obliquely, in the form of remedies for the situation rather than explicitly pointing out that the issue exists. For example, Jane points to the introduction of the GCSE in physical education as a positive development in her school: mainly because it helps in her quest to get physical education recognized by the senior management: 'now they've got to see us as not only sport, but as an education'. Pete, on the other hand, accepts the low status of his subject and himself, but on altogether different grounds. In his view, the 'educationist perspective' on physical education is the most intractable problem, leading to a downgrading of the practical sports element. He feels that a lack of recognition for pupils' abilities in practical activities and sports is, ultimately, the core of the status problem for physical education. Arnold also takes a pessimistic view, although for different reasons. He believes that within the secondary school culture, physical education teachers are seen as 'good disciplinarians' and 'good with kids', but are not really valued for anything else. This underpins his belief that he would need a further academic qualification in order to prove he has 'academic knowledge' in order to achieve promotion: 'The whole problem with teaching is everything is attached to your teaching subject.' The implication is that physical education is not academic at all. Laura, on the other hand, feels that she does have personal status because she is aware that she is held in high regard by senior staff. Even so, she feels that physical education gets a 'bad rap' from other teachers because of the 'old phys edder, sweaty jock' image. Like Arnold, Edgar's experience has taught him that physical educationists are seen as good disciplinarians. He perceives some hostility and a condescending attitude towards his subject from other staff in the school: 'I know some of them think of PE as just a chance for the kids to let off steam before they got back to some "real" work.' He has been particularly frustrated to find that other staff use physical education as a punishment:

'they'd exclude kids from the sports teams . . . just 'cos they couldn't control the kids. I found that really unfair'. Indeed, having fully bought into the notion of physical education as, centrally, a part of *education*, he has found the negative attitude of many in that education culture to be both baffling and wearing. This theme was echoed in Maggie's story. She initially questioned the title 'physical *education*', then answered her own question:

> I think it's because we have to try to justify ourselves beyond the public's image of sport being for the elite . . . in schools there's no other subject area that has to use the word 'education' to justify itself.

Finally, Grant pointed out that in three of the four schools in which he has taught, neither colleagues nor senior management have been supportive. He was particularly incensed when a new headteacher tried to persuade the physical education department to re-organize sports day as a 'fun' day. He felt that this reduced the work of the department to the level of trivia. Significantly, Grant identified the status issue as the most frustrating element of his work:

> . . . the real lows have just been the battles you fight against senior management within schools trying to get any kind of *fair play* towards physical education.

But how can this be? Why is physical education still striving for the basic right of 'fair play'; for acceptance as a full member of the education club? Does the fault lie with us in the physical education profession?

More About 'Us'

Writers in physical education have long argued the case for physical education to be a full member of the education community, as a sample of current and earlier literature demonstrates. Williams (1964) described physical education as 'an old and fundamental education' (p. 7) while Morgan (1974) noted that

> . . . the concept of physical education seems to demand that the values attaching to it shall integrate with those of the larger process of total education. A physically educated person must, by definition, be an educated person. (p. 86)

Myrle James (1967) pointed out that as members of the education group, physical education 'becomes responsible for the purposes to which the group is devoted' (p. 29) and more recently, Reid (1997) echoed both Morgan and Myrle James, noting that because physical education is a part of education 'its value must therefore be elucidated in terms of how it contributes specifically to, or reflects educational values in general' (p. 8). Carlisle (1977) outlined a vision of excellence, where physical education is viewed 'as primarily a mode of education' (p. 19) and he highlighted the potential of physical education:

> Physical education is a mode of education rich in subject matter and capable of being organised in an endless variety of programmes to suit the interests, aptitudes and temperaments of children of all ages. (p. 26)

Myrle James (1967) argued that physical education is indeed a part of education, unless teaching specific practical skills is the 'sole aim' of a physical education teacher. She concluded at that time that 'there are not many teachers of PE today who would willingly admit to this belief' (p. 2). Nor today, it would seem. Seven of the eight teachers in this book highlighted the educational nature of their roles and even Pete, whose philosophy often appears to be at odds with the other teachers, saw himself as an educator, albeit placing more emphasis upon specific practical outcomes. Lastly, Tinning et al. (1994) argue unequivocally that physical education 'needs to be conceptualised as an educational process, positioned within educational discourses and drawing upon educational argument' (cited in Macdonald and Brooker, 1997, p. 159).

So where does the problem lie? On the surface, at least, the physical education profession would appear to be *saying* all the right things to be a full member of the education club. Yet, at some level, it clearly isn't. Could it be the case that we are *saying* the right things but doing the 'wrong' things? If the 'wrong' things, in an educational context, are practical then we are in some difficulty. Fundamentally, we are just too practical and just too closely related to sport, as was noted in the last chapter. That, in a nutshell, is our crime. And whereas we have tried all sorts of approaches to show that physical education is 'more' than 'mere' sport, we have never taken that final step and distanced ourselves from the essential *practical* nature of our work. How could we? Without that, we would logically collapse as a 'physical' education. Morgan (1974) made the point, over 20 years ago, in the opening pages of a book with the surprisingly topical title: *Concerns and Values in Physical Education*:

> In a theoretical treatise it is well to make the point that physical education is not, in any fundamental sense, a theoretical subject. Like music, art and technology it is, in essence, practical. Theory in physical education, like

theory in art, music or technology may, at points, have general relevance but, on the whole, its function is to promote the performance and appreciation of practical work. (Foreword)

Not only is physical education an essentially practical subject, but physical education teachers are often proud of this. (Dowling Naess, 1996; Stroot et al., 1994). Moreover, the National Curriculum for England and Wales enshrines the practical focus in legal stone: 'The greatest emphasis should be placed upon the actual performance aspect of the subject' (DFE/WO, 1995, p. 2). So what can we do? As was noted earlier, the teachers in this book offered two possible 'status-solutions': emphasizing the links between physical education and 'health/fitness', and looking to the introduction of GCSE and 'A' level examinations to confer status.

Our Status-Solutions: Health and Fitness?

There is no doubt that, in the eyes of some in the profession, the holy grail of status lies in the actual or potential role of physical education in promoting health and fitness. This has a triple advantage in that it is clearly linked to the 'hard' sciences, it has an established and respected theoretical base, and it is topical in popular cultural terms (Fernandez-Balboa, 1995; Brooker and Macdonald, 1995). The teachers in this book seemed to view their roles as health/fitness teachers as 'natural'. For example, Grant wants pupils in physical education to be 'fit and healthy'. In his view, the best way to attain fitness is through specific sports activities, but if pupils don't find a sport in which they can participate, 'then, I suppose in a way we've failed and *I* haven't really achieved what I see as my objective for them'. Furthermore, he sees *fun* as a key measure of a department's success, suggesting that pupils should be disappointed if a lesson is cancelled and that involvement in sport after compulsory schooling is the ultimate test of success. Grant is, of course, identifying a notoriously difficult measure of success — the lifetime framework. He is not alone. Jane also saw her role as educating pupils for life after school, hoping that her pupils would 'see that they really have got fitness for life'. Pete saw health and fitness as important, based on his personal belief in 'the importance of staying fit and consequently healthy'. Arnold wanted to 'to promote a healthy lifestyle . . . to be able to direct individual skills to something fulfilling in terms of a sport that they can take up or follow' and Edgar commented that a good PE teacher should aim to encourage students to have a life-long interest in sport and physical activity, helping them to be fit and healthy. Maggie took a more pragmatic approach, pointing out that our aims in physical education are rather broad, and that try to do too much at times. Her compromise was that although lucation is important, we may have to settle for pupils 'understand-ing the whys' of health in physical education.

As with other topics, international research confirms that the teachers' views presented in this book are endorsed elsewhere. Stroot et al. (1994) report that many of their respondents saw 'exposure to lifetime activities and fitness with the hope of continued participation' (p. 349) as the central purpose of physical education. As one teacher commented: 'I think the major purpose of high school physical education is lifetime fitness' (p. 349). Not that there is universal agreement on the centrality of this element. Other teachers in Stroot et al.'s (1994) study described themselves as having broader social aims (see next chapter), and as Paul (1996) commented, the profession appears somewhat confused at times: 'We move from fitness activities to sport, we swing back to fitness, we call a moratorium on fitness, we discard physical education for wellness programs, etc.' (p. 541). That notwith-standing, it is difficult to find a definition of PE, either current or historical, which does not include health/fitness in some guise. For example, Morgan (1974) saw 'the promotion of fitness/health' as one of five 'concerns' in physical education; HMI (1989) identified an aim of physical education as 'to develop an understanding of the importance of exercise in maintaining a healthy life' (p. 2); the National Curriculum for England and Wales states that a general requirement for physical education is 'to promote physical activity and healthy life-styles' (DFE/WO, 1995); and Reid (1997) argues that education is fundamentally about human 'well-being' and that

> ... physical education's concern with the promotion of health is to be understood as a concern with the promotion of health-related knowledge, including practical skills, theoretical understanding, attitudes and habits. (p. 16)

Importantly, Reid (1997) also concludes that although it is a central value in physical education, health should not be considered 'the only value, or the dominant one' (p. 17), and this is certainly a theme which pervades the literature and the teachers' stories. In drawing together all the evidence, it seems reasonable to surmise that, notwithstanding critiques of individual-ism inherent in the health-related discourse (Colquhoun, 1989; Evans, 1989; Sparkes, 1989), it can be accepted that the inclusion of some form of health/fitness focus in physical education is a rare area of agreement in the profession. However, on the measure of raising status, the strategy would appear to have failed. Although there may have been some local successes, there is little or no consistent research evidence suggesting that a focus on health/fitness has significantly overcome status problems for physical education. But why is this?

The clues are probably in two pieces of evidence. The first of the Maggie's comment, cited earlier, that we may be trying to do too much physical education, and that we may need to be clearer about what we can actually achieve. Hence her more cautious aim to educate pupils in the 'whys' of fitness. Harris and Cale (1997) support this educational role for physical education:

> There is no doubt that the PE profession has a key role to play in promoting physical activity, in providing appropriate exercise guidance, and empowering young people to make informed exercise choices. (p. 59)

They would go further than Maggie, however, in that they feel physical education lessons should also be more active, to enhance health-benefits. Although several other teachers in this book could support that, Maggie might question the feasibility of the ideal.

The second is some recent research which supports Maggie's pessimism, and takes it even further. Curtner-Smith, Kerr and Clapp (1996) conducted case-study research on the teaching of health-related fitness. They found little existing research on the impact of the health-related element of the National Curriculum for Physical Education and none on the impact of that element on pupils' activity levels in PE lessons. They concluded from their five case-study schools that little if any positive impact on pupils' fitness could be ascertained and, moreover, that there was little in the curriculum which

> ... contributed to pupils' comprehension of the long- and short-term impacts of physical activity on their bodies or enabled them to make informed choices on where to focus their participation in physical activity for a healthy lifestyle. (p. 80)

Although the authors suggest that further research is needed to confirm the generalizability of these cases, one implication of their findings is that even Maggie's cautious aims might be overstated. If this is the case, then the education 'club' might have some grounds upon which to discount — or simply ignore — the health/fitness claims of physical educationists. Perhaps we have to accept that we simply don't have the time to deliver our health/ fitness aspirations, impressive though they sound, and that this is evident to everyone but ourselves anyway. The point is not new. Myrle James' (1967) charge still seems appropriate: 'Too many wild claims have been made in the past about the general effects of physical education' (p. 77).

A summary to this section appears to read as follows: we see health/ fitness as a 'natural' element of our work; we like it; and we feel it could be a 'status-solution'. On the other hand: we can't actually achieve very much in the time we have with pupils; we also have other important goals; it doesn't appear to be working as a 'status-solution'; but we ought to keep trying. As was noted at the beginning of this chapter — we are certainly persistent.

Our Status-Solutions: The Examination!

Apart from the health/fitness status-solution, the other solution offered by the case-study teachers was 'examinations'. Specifically, the teachers were referring to public examinations taken at the ages of 16 (GCSE) and 18 ('A' Levels) in Physical Education and/or Sport Studies. Interestingly for an essentially practical subject, it was the *theory* inherent in such examinations which was of interest to the teachers, primarily because it seemed to challenge them and impress colleagues. For example, Jane was particularly pleased that the GCSE syllabus entailed a lot of theory as she felt that it was only by teaching and examining *theory* that status could be earned. Like Jane, Diane thought that examinations were the route to status: 'it gives more status to teach it' and for Laura an examination was important because 'academically, we've proven that we're a subject to be reckoned with'. Even Pete saw some value in the examinations, although he showed concern for, what he viewed as, the superficiality of the practical courses. Arnold put it very bluntly: 'we have got into examinations because it seems to justify our place a little more'. So, is this the answer?

Well, on the face of it, examinations might be helpful in the status battle. However, the physical education profession seems to be agreed that physical education is, essentially, a practical subject. That is now enshrined in the National Curriculum. So, some caution is warranted. If examinations are important for status, and it is the theory which gives them the status, then where is the value in the majority of the curriculum — the practical curriculum? Could it be that, in our efforts to be accepted in the education club, we are only succeeding in further undermining ourselves and our practical core?

The literature is somewhat divided on the issue of theory in physical education. Vickers (1992) argued that movement to a more theoretically driven curriculum would indeed help status and O'Sullivan, Siedentop and Tannehill (1994) point out that the introduction of a 'substantial cognitive component' to physical education programmes in Australia and New Zealand has had a positive status outcome:

> ... a growing number of teachers perceive that they are viewed as legitimate professionals by their colleagues and that they have been more successful in their arguments to school administration for more time and

> financial allocations . . . the cognitive emphases of these new courses of
> study have provided a 'certain legitimacy' for physical education in schools
> that had been lacking for most teachers during their careers. (pp. 427–8)

Schempp's (1993) case-study research reinforces the point: 'It was, however, the practical or pedagogical content knowledge valued by Steve that was rejected by his students and ignored by the administration and community' (p. 17). In one sense, then, the teachers in this book may be right. Pursuing the practical pathway appears to be an unwise career choice in the education context (an issue which is discussed in more detail in the next section of this chapter). Reid (1997) makes the case unequivocally:

> When educationally significant knowledge is understood, narrowly, as the
> kind of propositional or theoretical understanding which is valued for its
> illuminative power, then it seems clear that physical education must either
> try to become the kind of academic curriculum activity which seeks to
> promote such knowledge, or resign itself to a marginal position in educa-
> tion. (p. 10)

If, therefore, physical education teachers decide that it is time to accept the prevailing inevitability of the high status of theoretical knowledge, and to seek acceptance in the education club by becoming more theoretical, then what should that theory look like?

Unsurprisingly, we are not agreed on this as a profession either. Paul (1996) points out that in the history of the physical education profession, we have rarely been of one mind; rather 'we have merely had pockets of cohesion' (p. 541). That is certainly true of the present also. For example, Tinning (1991) argues that our search for an appropriate discourse for physical education 'should begin with some of the emancipatory concerns addressed by critical and postmodern pedagogies' (p. 17). Compare this with the discourse of the influential 'sport education' proponents whose main objective is to sustain pupils' interest in sport: 'to help students become competent, literate and enthusiastic sport participants and consumers' (Siedentop, 1987). Little room for an emancipatory discourse there! Nor, perhaps, for Penney and Evans' (1997) arguments against the government-led drive to privilege the 'PE as sport' discourse in England and Wales, or for Brooker and Macdonald (1995) who critique a similar sport-led discourse in Australia and, linked with it, moves to a burgeoning discourse of science in physical education. They attribute this to the high status of scientific knowledge and, as in many other countries, this is also reflected in the increasing popularity of Sport Sciences courses in higher education, which seem to have captured the hearts and minds of students and faculty alike. The problem for Brooker and Macdonald, resides in their belief that such knowledge has a powerful influence upon physical education teacher preparation courses, and that it leaves students with 'only a partial understanding of PE' (p. 108). Rather, they would argue for pedagogical and social/cultural discourses, which they view as essential in any complete understanding of PE. Like Tinning (1991), they envisage physical education courses which are 'truly educational' (p. 107) in the broadest terms.

Naturally, this is only a sample of the 'pockets of cohesion' in physical education today. The health/fitness knowledge claims discussed earlier would be another, as would the 'physical education as social education' claims discussed in the next chapter. There are undoubtedly others. The important point to make is that, in each case, the 'theory' which informs physical education, and which therefore would be taught in schools, would look rather different. But which one can achieve the status goal most effectively?

The easy answer is to head for science. In effect, that is what many teachers in England have done because the examinations at both GCSE and 'A' level tend to mirror the discipline-centred approaches of the Sport Sciences in universities. One of the 'A' levels, for example, even has the title Sport Studies. It is, of course, taught almost exclusively by physical education teachers. But surely we have argued that we are not 'sports teachers'. That there is some confusion about the nature of our subject is, perhaps, unsurprising. We seem unsure ourselves.

Carlisle (1977) discussed the prevailing physical education discourses of the time and concluded that the debates about sport/competition/human movement studies/academic approaches to movement were 'a fairly messy potage'. He suggested that the mess is:

> . . . partly self-inflicted because physical education people have not been clear enough about the meaning, nature and significance of the subject, nor alive to the potential of the mode. (p. 22)

The charge seems to stick, if the evidence presented in this book is representative. And yet Carlisle's comment points to another side to the story. He describes the mess as *partly* self-inflicted. So who else is responsible? Perhaps it is time to examine the broader education community — they who constitute the club itself?

More About 'Them'

Paul (1996) traces the history of physical education within an academic framework and identifies four 'absolutes' which underpin the dilemmas of the physical education profession. The first two are important here:

One absolute is that human movement in sport, dance, games and exercise is our core whether we teach the how or study the why. The second absolute, because physical activity has never been accepted in the same vein as other educational subjects, is that we have always been defensive about our position in education. (p. 541)

The key phrase from the above is 'never been accepted'. The profession has made attempts to 'fit' in, but it is probable that full acceptance has simply never been a possibility. The club won't let us all the way in — no matter how we contort ourselves! There is certainly a lot of research support for this view; for example, the following extracts from research into the lives and careers of physical education teachers is illuminating:

From Dowling Naess (1996)
[Sven] had not bargained for the hostile reception awaiting him in the staffroom at his new school. He met a teacher culture which was hard to penetrate and dominated by an 'old guard'. He found himself in a school where PE had extremely low status, received little funding and low priority in matters of timetabling and the like. (p. 46)

The school's administration never actively encouraged Sven to pursue in-service training, and when he needed their support following his 'demotion' as a result of changes in the law concerning teacher qualifications, none was forthcoming. (pp. 49–50)

From Schempp (1993)
I asked Steve if the principal would sacrifice a chemistry lab, a portion of the library or even an athletic facility to preserve the all-purpose room for physical education. He laughed. Steve understood the principal's message: Physical education rests firmly on the bottom of the subject-matter status ladder. (p. 12)

The message from the community and the school cultures appeared to be, time and time again, that physical education was not education. (p. 14)

The continual disruption left the impression that physical education was considered little more than a play period that could be interrupted without harm . . . the opportunity for Steve to function as a 'teacher-as-intellectual' was crushed in the omnipotent pressure from a multitude of varied and trivial tasks constantly set before him by students, colleagues and administrators. (p. 15)

From Moreira, Sparkes and Fox (1995)
I do feel other teachers are sort of stereotypical of what teachers are and they always say, if you can't teach an academic subject , then you can only teach PE. And that comes across sometimes in a staffroom. I dislike that

very much . . . They wouldn't put it up there as being a good subject really. (p. 127)

From Stroot et al. (1994)
A major concern of these teachers was the little support by faculty colleagues for physical education and the importance of their role in the overall education of high school youth . . . Jocko believed . . . 'They think about it [physical education] as a nonacademic subject — the stereotype of a PE teacher — just dumb jocks'. (pp. 335–6)

From Macdonald and Brooker (1997)
Physical educators' status and work contexts include poor physical conditions, resources and facilities; a lack of professional support and development opportunities; role conflict; routinization of work; sexism; and burdensome managerial interactions with students . . . An Australian study (Macdonald, 1995) has identified these conditions as indicative of the proletarianization of physical educators' work. (p. 158)

The evidence is compelling — more so because the examples selected span Europe, America and Australia. So, this is not merely a local issue, the experiences of teachers in this book can be located in both an historical context and a contemporary international framework. It would appear, for example, that despite recent initiatives in physical education, we remain largely where Myrle James (1967) placed us over 30 years ago: 'Physical education has progressed a long way from the days of drill . . . It has, however, one more big step to take in order to assume its proper place in the mobile mosaic known as education' (Introduction). Well, physical education has certainly taken some steps, but we've either taken all the wrong ones, and so haven't yet qualified for full membership of the education club, or we have misunderstood the situation at a more fundamental level. Perhaps we were never really going to qualify anyway. A worrying thought?

Kretchmar (1996) examines the place of what he terms 'movement and play' in higher education. His resulting analysis can be usefully applied to physical education in secondary schools. He notes, for example, that 'motor activity in the context of games and play has been called nonintellectual, nonacademic, nonessential and nonartistic' (p. 433). In questioning the validity of this 'unfriendly' description, Kretchmar describes a 'tournament' in education in which there are four 'games'. The first of these games is 'about being intellectual and how important understanding is. It pits the theoreticians against the practitioners . . . the thinkers in opposition to the performers' (p. 434). This game is won by the theoreticians: 'Understanding, after all, is the hallmark of the educated person' (p. 434) and thus physical activity is viewed as nonintellectual. Physical education also loses the second game, because although all the players in this game are skill or performance related, some of these skills, like writing or information technology skills, are considered to be reflective in nature. The skills promoted in physical education can be viewed as 'nonacademic', primarily because of their manual nature. In the third game, between useful and nonuseful learning, physical education loses again. Whereas some 'manual' skills have clear application 'to make life go better' others are considered to be 'frills, delights and mere recreations' (p. 435). But which team should physical education join?

> In the degree to which we see ourselves as promoters of fitness, teachers of good character, or stress reducers, we are inclined to join the team that champions utility. But in the degree to which we hope to promote movement as just meaningful and fun, we are inclined to join the team that focuses on play. As it turns out, we cannot decide which way to go. Some of us compete for Team Utility, others for Team Play. (pp. 435–6)

Finally we reach game four, in which 'we face the only other three time losers' (p. 435). The game is between those who promote artistic skills, and those who do not. As sport is not generally considered to be art, and is more usually associated with 'low culture and crass entertainment' (p. 437) then we lose that game also. The result: 'We are assigned a peripheral role in the academy' (p. 437).

The value of Kretchmar's (1996) analysis is that it highlights, somewhat starkly, the multi-layered nature of the status difficulties facing physical education teachers. It also seems to lend support to the view that there is a limited amount that the profession can achieve 'no matter how abstractly and eruditely we present ourselves' (p. 340). Kretchmar's solutions are twofold. He suggests that we may be justified in refusing to play the game at all. Perhaps we should give up our attempts to be 'loved' by the education community. However, if we are to continue to play — to seek full acceptance — then there are several steps we should take. The first of these is that we need to 'better describe skilful practice as a way of knowing' (p. 339). Secondly, we need to make a clearer case for the value of this way of knowing: 'in the world that emphasises time, space, force and touch, we lead students in a unique way of knowing that gives them the power to explore, discover, express, invent and create' (p. 339). Interestingly, some of Kretchmar's final comments seem to echo the closing comments from the last chapter:

> How delightfully ironic it would be if those who were once labelled nonintellectual and nonacademic helped to lead the way in academe to a richer, more human understanding of intelligence and a broader, more defensible notion of academics. (p. 340)

Furthermore, Ktretchmar is not the first to make this claim. For example, Myrle James (1967) pointed out that:

> A great deal more about the relationship between physical activity and mental development should be known so that physical education can play a full part, with proper understanding, in the stages of the unfolding of a child's thought and intelligence. (pp. 20–1)

But, as was asked in the previous chapter, could we be so bold?

So, How About 'We'?

Locke (1987) suggests that if we want to instigate change, 'the trick is to stop blaming people (others or ourselves) and start dealing with the human problems that limit what our programs might become' (p. 20). It seems like good advice. The physical education profession, like any good victim, has blamed itself endlessly. There is clearly some ground for self-chastisement, but it's not the whole story. The role of the broader education community in defining the low status of physical education, and in failing to challenge it, must also be understood. Without such an understanding, it is certainly tempting to think that physical education will achieve status — if only it finds the elusive status formula. Schempp (1993) cites Tomlinson's (1981) argument that there should be an ethos of collective responsibility for improving practice in schools. Such a responsibility could include an acknowledgment of the contribution to learning which each curriculum area can make. In this respect, Giroux's (1991) call for an appreciation of 'difference' in education could be helpful, particularly when it becomes clear that such an appreciation manifestly does not extend to the practical subject of physical education. Giroux argues for an inclusive discourse of 'border pedagogy' in education where:

> . . . educators can bring the concepts of culture, voice and difference together to create a borderland where multiple subjectivities and identities exist as part of a pedagogical practice that provides the potential to expand the politics of democratic community and solidarity. (p. 516)

Although Giroux's thoughts may not have been upon physical education when he wrote this, it does serve to highlight that notions of 'community' and 'solidarity' are far removed from most of the secondary school cultures encountered by teachers in this book. Rather, their experiences are closer to that noted by Stroot et al. (1994), who found very little support for physical education from other teachers and, furthermore, 'perceptions of physical education as a legitimate subject matter were non-existent' (p. 356). In Giroux's (1991) vision of a 'borderland', physical education teachers would appear to be very much 'on the borders', excluded from the 'solidarity' of the school community by virtue of their (practical) subject matter. O'Sullivan, Siedentop and Tannehill (1994) capture the circularity of the process thus:

> If the high school ecology marginalizes physical education and makes it difficult to change, certainly the manner in which physical education teachers and programs succumb to those contingencies makes it difficult for high school change agents to get physical education moving. (p. 426)

To remedy the situation, O'Sullivan et al. (1994) suggest that physical education teachers must promote themselves and their programs within the broader education community; and must also realize that 'The future depends *in part* on the role we define for ourselves' (p. 427, our emphasis).

There it is: 'in part'. It has been argued in this chapter that the broader education community must accept some responsibility for the low status of physical education, and that it is only in working together on the concept of 'we' — all teachers valuing the educational potential of all subjects — that any real change in the status of physical education will take place. And of course the range of doubters is even wider. O'Sullivan et al. (1994) point to the need to convince parents, pupils and the general public of the value and potential of physical education. We can certainly try. But if we want to get our message across, we need to be sure that someone is listening. That may be our first task. Then, once we have their attention, we need to be sure that we can deliver a consistent message, for the audience may well be sceptical and fickle. Finally, without further research into the educational potential of our practical activities, we are not in a position to deliver a consistent and defensible argument which justifies the practical teaching in which we are so visibly involved. So what are we waiting for?

Chapter 12

'Caring' in Physical Education:
A Three-dimensional Analysis

Introduction

> Children know whether you care, they know whether you're interested in them. (Laura's story)

The teachers in this book 'cared' about their pupils, albeit in different ways and about different things. For many, notions of 'caring' were inextricably linked to the ideal of using physical education, and particularly sport, as a form of social and moral education. Indeed, this could be identified as a third attempt at a 'status-solution' for physical education, to join the two already identified in the previous chapter: health/fitness knowledge claims and the privileging of theoretical knowledge. However, just like those solutions, the attempt to gain status by claiming a special role in pupils' social and moral education appears to have failed; the status mountain is still to be conquered (Macdonald and Brooker, 1997). But why has it failed?

The teachers' stories highlighted some laudable social/moral aspirations for pupils, and there was an overriding feeling that physical education could offer something unique in this area, either in terms of a special teacher–pupil relationship, special subject matter or a special learning environment. Furthermore, the optimism of these teachers appears to be shared by others (O'Sullivan et al., 1994; Dowling Naess, 1996). Yet, there was also some confusion evident. It was difficult to quantify the precise nature of teachers' aspirations for pupils' social and moral development but, like health and fitness knowledge claims, they just seemed to feel it was a 'natural' part of their work. The senior management team at Citylimits High School were largely in agreement (Armour, 1996). The evidence from this study seems to suggest that, somehow, physical education is seen as a context for 'caring' about pupils and, as a consequence, for enhancing pupils' social and moral skills. But how?

This chapter explores the issue in, what we identify as, the three dimensions of caring in physical education. Firstly, 'caring', as expressed by the case-study teachers is considered in the light of Noddings' (1984) analysis of caring in education. This includes a consideration of the ways in which individual teachers have developed an ethic of care and how they have resolved crises in their careers which threatened their ability to care for pupils. As a result of this analysis, the notion of a 'child centred' philosophy for physical education is questioned. Secondly, the claim that physical education and sport have a particular social and moral value in pupils' education is examined because, by implication, it follows that physical education *teachers* have a unique caring responsibility. However, many of these claims rest on the assumption that sport is, in some way, a character building activity. Unfortunately, there is little research evidence to support this and so the claim is difficult to defend. Finally, the influence of powerful role models in the lives of the case-study teachers is detailed and the educational potential of 'the sporting environment' is considered. In an ironic finale, the 'high points' of teaching, as expressed in the teachers' stories, are compared with the other claims they have made about their roles as teachers and for the value of their subject. The two don't match, and this raises the interesting possibility of the existence of a fourth dimension — rhetoric aside — that they *really* care about.

The First Dimension: The 'Caring' Teacher of Physical Education

As was noted earlier, it was obvious that most, if not all, of the case-study teachers expressed an ethic of care in the interviews. This was, however, demonstrated in a variety of ways and to differing degrees. In order to provide a reference point for the analysis, we decided to use the framework of Nell Noddings' (1984) definitive work on caring in education. However, in applying the concepts to the teachers' stories, we sought to avoid suggestions that there are, somehow, universal concrete rules about the nature of 'good' caring. It isn't that simple. Consider comments by some of the case-study teachers:

> As far as I'm concerned, it's for the kids; it's for the kids who like doing PE. The kids are the best indicator [of a good programme]. (Grant)

> The educationalists would say you have to teach the group — I say, that's what you're trying to do, but you're failing. You're not really getting cricket over to the people who are potentially cricketers, and they're suffering because you're having to spend pro-rata more time on those who are totally disenchanted — well out of love with cricket. Be satisfied with those people who are not really going to reach a good standard, and really get into those who you can perhaps see are going to make cricketers, and get some excellence. (Pete)

It's about giving the children a worthwhile experience. It's about filling them with confidence, it's filling them with a range of experiences. It's giving them . . . a love of something. (Laura)

One of the best pieces of advice I was ever given was from the deputy head at my last school, and he said, 'Laura, in these children's lives, we're some of the most constant things. They know in the morning when they come in that you'll still be there for them, whereas when they go home at night they don't know what's happening'. Children know whether you care, they know whether you're interested in them. If you're interested in them, they're interested in your subject. (Laura)

I do want the best for the kids, and I think you've got to be prepared to use the best method regardless of whether it's on the right bandwagon at the time. (Maggie)

On first analysis, it appears that the teachers fundamentally cared about pupils as individuals. Indeed, this is a central tenet of Noddings' (1984) philosophy:

. . . the actions of one caring will be varied rather than rule-bound, that is, her (sic) actions, while predictable in a global sense, will be unpredictable in detail . . . to act as one caring, is to act with special regard for the particular person in a concrete situation. (p. 24)

Such views echo those of Kegan (1982) in psychology, who believes that the twin themes of relationship/connection and autonomy/independence should be used to conceptualize human development (Rovegno and Kirk, 1995). Similarly, many of the teachers in this book expressed a desire to instil autonomy in pupils, as reflected in increased self-confidence and self-esteem, within a framework of interdependence and teamwork. Although the twin themes of self-confidence and teamwork were recurring ones, the wider notion of 'caring' was expressed in different, and sometimes con-flicting ways. Care ranged from Jane's concern to foster pupils' long-term interest in health, to Pete's aim of helping all pupils, and in particular the better athletes achieve their full potential in sport. Pete's emphasis on promoting excellence in competitive sport has, until very recently, been unfashionable in education and this has left him open to criticisms of not caring. On the contrary, Pete cares very much; he just seems to care about different things. Furthermore, he is undoubtedly a committed teacher, and his passion for his beliefs was only matched, perhaps, by Laura's convic-tion about her beliefs. Indeed, all the teachers cared passionately about something, confirming the earlier point: it is impossible to make qualitative judgments about 'good' and 'bad' caring. Therefore, although a broad ethic of care, or at least a verbal commitment to caring, was readily evident, we felt we needed to know more about the specifics of the caring role of the teacher in physical education.

'Relationality'; i.e. being in relation to others involving caring and being cared for, is central to Noddings' (1984) framework. Such caring is grounded in 'feelings, needs, impressions and a sense of personal ideal', with the roots of such behaviour being 'located in affective human response' (Noddings, 1984, p. 3). In the context of physical education, Macdonald and Brooker (1995) argue that in order to establish a truly emancipatory pedagogy, caring for the needs of the learner must be present in the guises of emotional sensitivity and critical insight. At the heart of such an ethic lies both responsibility and relationship. It would seem, then, that the *actuality* of caring in physical education is a caring based on the deeper concept of relationality. Arnold's story raises some interesting questions in this respect. He is an individual who is credited, in the school culture that is Citylimits High School, as a caring education professional. However, he made it clear that he cares little for physical education and, by implication, the pupils in it. He even admitted: 'I wouldn't have thought that any of my PE lessons were ... particularly, where I felt "that was really good, that was. I achieved a great deal in that time",' and he was constantly searching for the wherewithal to 'get out', both of physical education and education. Meanwhile, he stays in post, focuses upon pastoral work and is despondent. It is difficult to see how Arnold can care deeply about pupils; he is too preoccupied with his own concerns — not that this is a criticism.

Noddings (1984) provides an explanation which seems to clarify Arnold's position, and also the actions of some of the other teachers. If the caring is incomplete, in that the act of caring is rejected by the cared for, the caring often turns into 'cares and burdens' (Noddings, 1984). The caring, as a consequence, turns inward with the focus being shifted to the carer and his or her worries. Such a downward spiral could be initiated by, for example, intolerable conditions or difficult pupils. One of the case-study teachers, Edgar, provides a good example of the latter. To borrow from Martin Buber's (1970) concept of 'Thou and I', in Edgar's case, the cared-for 'thou' (subject) became an 'it' (object) as, overwhelmed by the responsibility of his task, he became the focus of his own caring. This is not to say that Edgar didn't care for the pupils at this time. He cared enough to take the decision to resign, thus ending a state of conflict and frustration which could have left him open to the accusation that 'he doesn't care'. In line with Noddings' (1984) belief in the double requirement of courage in caring, Edgar took the decision to withdraw due to his own 'cares and burdens', re-evaluated his priorities, and had the courage to re-enter the profession; that is, to care again. Since resigning his post at Enterprise High, Edgar has recovered his enthusiasm and is back teaching, albeit on supply. Noddings explains it thus: 'I recognise that I do not care at this time, that I am weary, but I recognise also, that this mood may pass' (p. 37). Interestingly, Jane's story provides yet another example of an individual who felt that her caring, in this case for her subject above all else, was not respected by the broader education community. She felt that they were more interested in a range of nebulous educational initiatives which detracted from her time for physical education: 'It's not the teaching . . . [but] all this new jargon and administration is really too much and is really not for me.' As a result, she too has left her post and is currently enjoying a post in further education where she can focus upon physical education in a way that she finds acceptable. By contrast, Arnold has been unable to resolve his 'cares and burdens'. Perhaps he needs to take a tip from Edgar and Jane.

Pete was also disillusioned. Again, this could be attributed to the difference between what he cared about — pupils in sport — and the priorities of the school. However, Pete's reaction was different to that of Jane and Edgar, in that he stayed in post; and it was qualitatively different to that of Arnold, in that he enjoyed his work. It was evident, for example, that Pete retained immense enthusiasm for his daily role with pupils in physical education, even though he was very pragmatic about what he could achieve with pupils. In fact, and in a reflection of Noddings' (1984) philosophy, Pete appears to believe that, in the long run, pupils will only learn what they please. As Noddings puts it: 'what he (sic) makes his own and eventually applies effectively, is what he finds significant for his own life' (p. 176). He therefore considers it pointless to treat all pupils alike, in that 'not everyone wants the same thing' (Pete's story). In some ways, Pete is the most realistic (dare we say honest?) of the teachers in the book. No conflict seemed apparent between what he said he wanted the pupils to achieve, and what he taught. He worked for concrete goals with the pupils, which were directly related to skill mastery and competitive success. Such clarity and consistency between means and ends was refreshing, even though Pete's views were, at times, elitist and chauvinistic, and were considered as such by many of the other staff at Citylimits. Thus, although he can be viewed as a traditional macho male physical education teacher, his philosophy of trying to help pupils achieve what *they* want, could be viewed as being tailored to individual needs; even child-centred (although Jane and Arnold might not agree!). This would seem to mirror Noddings' (1984) philosophy that the role of the teacher should be to influence and to put his or her energy at the *service* of the student. The caring approach, then, is very much a child-centred one.

Yet, there's more to it. As was noted at the beginning of this chapter, it was obvious that, in their own ways, the teachers in this book cared for pupils and their learning. However, further analysis of the interviews raises some interesting questions about the vehicle for promoting the caring ethic. For example, it is was apparent that most of these teachers wanted the children to learn and develop desirable social and character traits from involvement in the activities of physical education, particularly sport. They identified this as the vehicle more readily than they identified themselves as social/moral leaders. The onus, thus, appears to be upon the activity to do most of the educating (a concept discussed in the next section) while their roles as teachers lay in motivating the pupils to take part. Penney and Evans (1997) might take issue with this view:

> The needs and interests of children are not, of course, likely to be met through their relationship with an activity alone. Development, whether in sport or PE, has to be mediated and nurtured by good teaching and the actions of individuals well trained, imbued with sophisticated pedagogical skills. (p. 25)

Yet the case-study teachers seemed rather shy about detailing their own personal roles in the social and moral education of pupils, even though they saw this a central function of physical education itself. Perhaps, in some cases, they were able to care 'about' pupils but, in Noddings' (1984) terms, were unable to care 'for' them. Certainly, all cared 'about' the pupils in general terms: for example, wanting to give them 'fitness for life', or sports they could follow after school. At this level of generality, their aspirations were not exceptional and could be matched by other teachers in various ways in their own subjects. So this is not unique to physical education. In order to claim that the caring in physical education is qualitatively different, the profession would need to demonstrate that such caring is more akin to caring 'for', as Noddings' expresses it. Thus, the caring would need to be demonstrated at a deeper individualistic level reflected, perhaps, in being available for all pupils as individuals, and establishing deep relationships with each of them. But how is this possible? Perhaps the philosophy is flawed.

Sugrue (1997) argues that a child-centred approach which focuses on pupils' individual needs must also recognize 'that its implications for teaching are problematic' (p. 11). Pring (1976) went further, questioning the whole concept of 'child-centredness', suggesting instead that teachers teach what they want to teach — albeit using the needs of pupils as a justification. Hirst (1974) put it bluntly: 'Saying what children need is only a cloaked way of saying what we judge they ought to have' (p. 16) and Appleyard (1991) points out that although the aims of a child-centred education might be laudable, they are rarely applied rigorously, resulting in an education system which is characterized by 'caring blandness' (p. 12). The teachers' stories in this book seem to support Pring's scepticism. Analysis of their life-stories makes it abundantly clear that their philosophies for physical education were certainly child-centred, but the 'child' at the root of their philosophies was usually themselves and their own childhood experiences. Nor are physical education teachers peculiar in this respect. Interviews with the senior management team at Citylimits High School revealed that each individual's aspirations for physical education within education were demonstrably and unashamedly based on personal experiences of sport and physical education during childhood (Armour, 1996). The resulting ethic of care was certainly not 'bland' however. Rather more problematically, it was powerful and largely immutable. But perhaps it was not pernicious in any way. Sugrue (1997) puts it well:

> The principles of child-centredness are ambiguous for classroom action and are, therefore, problematic. However, the seamless tapestry of their sentiment admits no such ambiguity. *In an uncritical moment, it can be said that child-centred ideology has its heart in the right place.* The sentiment arouses different passions in practitioners, which are tempered by personal biography, professional experience and local circumstance. (p. 22, our emphasis)

Certainly, the teachers' stories in this book would support Sugrue's claim, particularly the point about personal biography, and about 'local circumstance', which is important in physical education and is discussed later in this chapter. But there is more to it. In addition to the caring teacher, there was a suggestion that the subject matter itself is unique, and it is in this second dimension that many of the social/moral knowledge claims for physical education are located.

The Second Dimension: The Social/Moral Value of Physical Education and Sport

There is no doubt that the teachers in this book were keen to make a social/moral knowledge claim for physical education. Consider some of their comments:

> I think that PE can also raise the confidence of kids, especially those who aren't really academic . . . it's definitely an area for self-expression and to develop feelings of self-worth and self-confidence. We should try to include the social aspect (even) more, in that we should help kids understand that they need others to get on in life. The games should be conditioned for maximum involvement. (Edgar)

You learn anyway when you play sport — like to interact with other people and taking responsibility in, for example, a team. (Diane)

I see my role and the role of my subject as to enhance their (children's) self-esteem . . . to make them feel like they've got something to offer be it individually or in a group . . . it's preparing them for the world beyond. (Laura)

We're using [sport] as a vehicle to open up a lot of other avenues. A lot of the things that apply in netball they can apply elsewhere, not just in games, but they can apply elsewhere in life as well. By relating to people in a sporting context, you learn how to relate to people in life, in general. (Maggie)

The debate over the appropriate role of sport, physical education and physical activity within a wider social context seems always to have been with us. As was noted in Chapters 10 and 11, these debates hinge upon the different status of 'mind' and 'body' in education (Reid, 1997). Indeed, current perceptions regarding the purpose and status of contemporary physical education can be traced back to the philosophers of fourth century BC in Athens, and in particular to Socrates, his pupil Plato, and his pupil Aristotle. It was here that the belief in the dualistic nature of existence, dividing reality into the twin components of mind and body, was nurtured and developed (Mechikoff and Estes, 1993). Such a philosophy was emphasized to a much greater degree by the Ascetics of the Middle Ages, who based their further degradation of anything physical on the concept of original sin. Physical activity within Western culture has thus always had to be justified in terms of non-physical gains, be it an appropriate physique to house the more important cognitive function, or for the development of desirable moral and social traits.

In relation to that philosophy, the belief that involvement in games could develop character was an integral aspect of the 'muscular Christianity' movement, which took firm root in the nineteenth-century English public school system. Instrumental in this development were headteachers such as Arnold at Rugby and Cotton of Harrow: 'who stressed the value of sport in creating order in schools, which earlier in the century had experienced revolts by pupils' (Holt, 1992, p. 21). Indeed, since masters in the nineteenth-century public schools of England took charge of the games for pupils, the notion that sport is an agent of socialization and social control has been widely espoused. Thus, Wellington's alleged comment about the 'battle of Waterloo being won on the playing fields of Eton' has been echoed by teachers, coaches and the media who claim that desirable character traits can be fostered through participation in physical education, games and sports.

The belief in sport as a builder of character was, therefore, an ideological construct employed in educational settings to promote useful qualities for the expanding imperialistic British empire of the nineteenth century. Such qualities included self-confidence, fortitude, loyalty, determination and bravery among others (Sheilds and Bredemeier, 1995). It was through sport and games that the ideology was both constructed and sustained; involvement in physical activity becoming the means to a greater social end. The philosophy was further reinforced by the existing class structure of the time and the related belief in 'amateurism'. Thus, it was, that sport was believed to build character, only if it remained a non-serious leisure activity; the implication being that if profit could be won, moral gains could not.

The belief in sport as an agent of socialization is grounded in the philosophy that games develop an 'enculturative outcome' (Sutton-Smith, 1973, p. 2), whereby participants develop transferable skills relevant to survival and achievement in the wider society. Indeed, this notion of sport as a character builder has traditionally been at the core of justifications offered for the existence of physical education and sport in educational institutions (Stevenson, 1975). Additionally, philosophers such as Arnold (1984) have conceptualized the sport/education argument in terms of 'moral self-formation', in that through participating, personal responsibility for how the practice of sport is conducted is accepted, leading to a developed sense of self-respect and confidence. Arnold's philosophy is based on the belief that sport is founded upon the moral principles of freedom and equality: freedom in the respect that those who partake, do so of their own volition, and equality in that by choosing to participate they commit themselves to a given set of rules applicable to all. Consequently, he concludes that 'because sport embodies moral principles, it can be a productive place for the practice of moral virtue' (Sheilds and Bredemeier, 1995, p. 174) His belief that sport should be understood as a valued human activity and should therefore be taught for its own sake (a radical philosophy for some of the teachers in this book), is contextualized by his valuation of sport as an inherently moral practice. This provides the justification for his adherence to a philosophy of sporting involvement.

However, if one questions the assumption of sport as being inherently moral, as many have done to good effect (why should sport be lumbered with such a monstrous burden?), then the case for social/moral learning is weakened. For example, little research evidence exists which supports the contention that sport builds character, with many authors counter-claiming that it does the exact opposite (Oglivie and Tutko, 1971; Miracle and Rees, 1994; Lee, 1996). Proponents of such a belief have argued that an over-emphasis on competitive outcomes promotes anti-social behaviour and generates moral problems (Orlick, 1990). Others contend that sport mirrors the negative values of the wider culture in which it occurs (Sage, 1990; Talbot, 1996). On a different note, critical theorists such as Sage (1990), have argued that sport has been, and continues to be used as a vehicle of socialization, and that the 'real achievement of organised sport programmes is training participants to accept the prevailing social structure'(p. 200). It is also obvious that many athletes learn and are taught to break the rules in sport. Indeed, in some cases, as in the closing stages of many top-level basketball games, rule breaking has actually become part of game strategy. If such practice is condoned (and in the example given it obviously is), the sporting experience may be providing reinforcement for values that are antithetical to the character building ideals generally espoused for sport (Sage, 1990).

The existing body of research does not appear to conclusively support either position, with possibly a more insightful conclusion being that the question regarding sport as a builder of character is, in its existing form, too simplistic (Sheilds and Bredemeier, 1995). As Sheilds and Bredemeier argue, the vagueness of the term 'character' and the difficulty of defining the role of sport in this context, have hampered investigation and precluded meaningful findings on the issue. Yet, we in the physical education profession still make the social and moral claims, as a glance at the teachers' case-study stories confirms. For them, participation in sport does, or can, build desirable social and moral traits. Perhaps this is unsurprising given that the teachers came, almost exclusively, from a generation that experienced physical education both as secondary school children and college students in the 1970s and 1980s. During this time, the influence of the humanistic discourse was at its height and this seems to lend support to claims about the political nature of physical education, and the suggestion that its fluctuating disposition influences teaching values and practices (Rovegno and Kirk, 1995; Macdonald and Brooker, 1995; Penney and Evans, 1997).

An earlier analysis by Morgan (1974) provides an interesting perspective on the debate. He acknowledges both positions — for and against the notion of sport as a character building activity — but suggests that it is a lack of experimental evidence which prevents the issue from being resolved. Interestingly, it is a claim which reverberates throughout this book. Morgan also makes some insightful observations:

> There seems to be no conceivable reason why a child should not apprehend moral concepts of a general value — and cement them in practice — during his involvement in games . . . this is no more than stating a conviction, based on rational thought, that games can, under certain circumstances, serve useful experience in moral education or character training. Whether they do commonly serve this purpose, in any significant measure, is a different question. (pp. 75–6)

117

> If we believe that extrovert tendencies can be reinforced with good effect through a particular form of training we must surely admit that the process can be carried to excess . . . No medium is of any value in moral education which is not at the same time potentially dangerous. The situations which present opportunities for truly brave or kind acts are those which also present alternatives; not only for the direct opposites, cowardice or selfishness, but for all kinds of excesses, evasion or pretences which may be morally harmful. Much that passes for sport these days, both professional and amateur, is brutal, dishonest and utterly selfish. (pp. 78–9)

Most significantly, perhaps, Morgan (1974) makes the fundamental point that for any moral education to take place, 'the guidance must be there, the personal example and, occasionally, the precept' (p. 75). The suggestion is, surely, that the activity cannot shoulder the burden of moral leadership — not alone at least — there is a major role for the teacher. As Penney and Evans (1997) pointed out earlier, there is no substitute for good teaching. But, as was also noted earlier, teachers seemed a little reticent about placing themselves in the role of moral leadership. Rather, they sought to provide maximum opportunities for pupils to partake in sports and physical activity, and by so doing, seemed to hope that they would 'catch' desirable social values. Yet, as their own life-stories made clear, the role of *their* physical education teachers was much more proactive than that.

The Third Dimension: Caring Role-models in a Sporting Environment

Judging by their comments, most of the teachers in this book had encountered teachers who had truly cared 'for' them, and who met Noddings' (1984) exacting caring criteria of 'relationality' and 'dialogue'. Role-models were, then, caring teachers who 'invested a great deal of themselves in the school . . . they give everything to the job' (Moreira, Sparkes and Fox, 1995, p. 131). In several of the stories, a hero or heroine figure is evident:

> Do you know, now that I'm sitting down talking about it I just think how lucky I've been. It's the fact that they [her physical education teachers] loved their job enough to want to give up numerous, numerous — not just like a Saturday — we went away for weekends upon weekends. (Maggie)

> Oh they were brilliant! Absolutely brilliant. Jack I suppose was the one who had the most impact on me . . . he was such a nice person, I mean, when I failed one of my exams he gave me a big hug as he was so upset for me . . . And Tracy, she was really good, she was so *loud* . . . and we

got on really well and she helped me a lot . . . we were just really, really friendly and I could chat to them and go down and help them. (Diane)

He was a good man, he really helped kids out. (Pete)

The PE teachers there were very committed, very good sportsmen in their own right. They were always available, lunchtimes and after school practices and that sort of thing. I suppose even at that time, I looked up to them as role models, as I said, as fit, committed people. (Arnold)

On the other hand, there were also some disappointing teacher role-models:

Why do you think I am like I am in wanting my children to achieve? . . . What happened to a lot of children I went to school with was that the teacher didn't really care, so they stopped caring. (Laura)

Now that I think back to it I really feel a bit angry and frustrated because I feel had I ever got taught or coached when I was a bit younger, I might have been better at something. (Grant)

Both positive and negative influences were recalled vividly in the interviews, with their importance in current philosophies clearly evident. Where bad practice had been encountered, teachers seemed even more determined that their pupils would receive a better experience. Alternatively, the positive role-models were referred to in glowing, inspirational terms, as people to emulate. Their comments seem to reinforce Noddings' (1984) recognition of 'relatedness', which forms the foundation of her care ethic and also her suggestion that much of what is valuable in the teaching–learning relationship cannot be specified, although an attitude characteristic of caring emerges through acquaintance. Thus, when a pupil associates with a teacher feeling free to initiate conversation, a smile or eye-contact may convey to the former that 'I am (still) interested in you', boosting the process of self-actualization (Noddings, 1984). As outsiders, we can only catch glimpses of the depth of the teacher–pupil relationships described by the teachers in this book. Even so, it is hard to miss their power.

It is also difficult to dismiss the significance of the 'local circumstance' (Sugrue, 1997) of physical education within the broader school culture. The sporting environment, within a physical education framework, appears to provide fertile ground for caring relationships, such as those detailed above, to flourish. This environment, especially in relation to changing room banter and interaction, seems to provide a unique backdrop against which meaningful individualistic relationships with pupils can be developed. It is also clear that the establishment of such relationships is viewed as very close to the essence of teaching by many of the teachers within this book, as it was also the essence of their own education. According to Noddings (1984), a teacher's highest priority is to 'nurture the student's ethical ideal' (p. 178). Teachers generally are in a unique position to do this, as they are in contact with this ideal as it is being constructed, and through dialogue and commitment can influence and 'encourage the student to stand personally by what he (sic) says and does' (p. 178). The purpose of dialogue is to meet and understand the other, while extended contact is likely to result in deeper relationships. In physical education, there is ample opportunity for the softening of formal barriers, potentially allowing meaningful and caring relations between students and staff to be established. Moreover, the 'sporting environment' itself is particularly opportune in this context; and it was experienced as such by several of the teachers — consider Maggie's story, for example. Connell (1985) identified this phenomenon, noting the more relaxed relationship a physical education teacher had with the children in comparison to teachers from other 'academic' (sic) subjects. He suggested, although did not develop, the notion that 'the different setting of his work' was the reason (p. 74). O'Sullivan et al.'s (1994) research reinforces the point:

> . . . their gymnasia and offices were quite livable places where these teachers had established wonderful social relationships with students. It was common for several teachers to have small groups of smiling and happy students in their offices before and after physical education lessons who bantered with each other and the teachers. (p. 425)

Noddings (1984) stresses the need to preserve the uniqueness of human encounters, and to direct efforts 'towards the maintenance of conditions that will permit caring to flourish' (p. 5). Time spent in the changing room before lessons 'chatting, cheeking' (Pete's story) establishes just such conditions; an informal environment almost unique within the school setting. Certainly for the teachers in this book, the fond memories and bonds established with their own physical education teachers remained as powerful reminders of what could be achieved — or not. Jane felt some regret that she was unable to develop relationships with pupils to match those she developed with her own teachers.

So, is this the very core of physical education? The evidence from these teachers, and from a range of literature, suggests that the physical education profession values its social and moral knowledge claims, which are developed through the three dimensions of caring teachers, inherently moral subject matter and a particular teaching and learning environment. More empirical support for these claims would not go amiss. As for them representing the very core of physical education — well, perhaps. But in the final stages of the interviews with the case-study teachers, a fourth dimension of 'caring' appeared — as if from nowhere — and it had little or nothing to do with pupils' social/moral education.

What Did the Teachers Really *Care* About?

Well, we can only make assumptions. But in the final stage of the interviews, each teacher was asked to identify the 'high points' of teaching. Their comments seem to speak volumes:

> In tennis for example, all of a sudden, they've [the pupils] got it. They've turned and done it properly, and I've found myself shouting 'Yeh, that's brilliant!' ... And when my team started to be successful this year ... I could see they had potential, but it needed a lot of work and this year, all of a sudden it clicked! ... it was such a good feeling to have a winning team that I'd worked with and they'd improved so much. (Diane)

> The good things are, basically, it's having a good lesson — when you've taught a lesson and the kids have worked well, and actually, sometimes you can see a definite progression, a definite development of skill over the course of only one hour ... and then over the course of five or six weeks, if things have gone really well, that for me, has been the high points of teaching. (Grant)

> I think when you have a successful team. That can make you feel pretty good. But personally, I'll always remember [a pupil] who was pretty uncoordinated, and I used to encourage this girl as much as I possibly could in all the lessons, and she improved so much that that really made me feel on a high. (Jane)

> ... not just in rugby but anything ... because that's where I see a lot of hard work has been put in after school, which is of my own volition, no-one's forcing me to do it and that's where it really comes through. That's a high for me. (Pete)

> This is going to sound really awful, I mean I enjoy my lessons, but I love my extra-curricular. (Maggie)

It is ironic. When asked about physical education in abstract terms, the teachers gave responses which emphasized a range of knowledge claims for physical education, as presented earlier in this and in the previous chapter. They clearly felt that such claims were impressive and would enhance status in the sceptical education culture. They were, of course, using 'strategic rhetoric' (Sparkes, 1987), and they have, of course, failed in their status quest. On the other hand, when asked about the 'high points' of teaching, the rhetoric evaporates and, it could be argued, the essence of the subject emerges. What most of these teachers of physical education *really* seem to care about, is the physical. Whether it be pupils who try hard, as in the case of Jane; pupils who have the potential to be successful, as in the case of Pete; or, as Grant suggested, pupils who progress over a six-week block of work, it is the visible, almost measurable improvements in pupils' physical aptitude which makes teaching worthwhile — which is, thus, the essence of physical education. The tragedy, is that so few of the teachers had the confidence to place this at the centre of their explanations about the purpose and value of physical education. They are, perhaps, acutely aware that the education club ('Them', in Chapter 11) would be largely unimpressed: would demand more.

Yet again, it seems, a chapter ends with the status issue in a pivotal position. Maggie's final apologetic comment speaks volumes. She felt she had to apologize for most enjoying that part of her work where some pupils volunteer to do *more* of her subject, and where they try to do exceptionally well. Could it happen in any other subject? It is, in a nutshell, the conflict inherent in the contemporary physical education teacher's lived experience.

Chapter 13

Moving In, Moving Along and Moving Out: Career Progression in Physical Education

Introduction

There is relatively little literature on physical education teachers and their careers. What does exist tends to paint a picture of an occupation in turmoil, in which career satisfaction is rarely achieved (Sparkes, Templin and Schempp, 1990; Templin, Sparkes and Schempp, 1991). However, some literature also suggests that satisfaction is possible (Rog, 1986), particularly where individuals 'understand the contextual and personal struggles of (their) lives and careers' (Templin, Sparkes, Grant and Schempp, 1994, p. 275). Nevertheless, it appears that if teachers are to successfully negotiate a rewarding career in the profession, they need to be adept at addressing a myriad of contextual workplace, status and support issues. This will come as no surprise to those who have read the previous two chapters. Inevitably, the interaction between and within these contextual variables significantly impinges on teachers' commitment to their work and, unsurprisingly, previous studies have concluded that such commitment varies, over a career span, for innumerable personal and professional reasons (Sikes, Measor and Woods, 1985; Moreira et al., 1995). Thus, taking Yee's (1990) definition of a satisfying career 'as one (in) which individuals seek to experience a sense of achievement and accomplishment during the course of their work' (p. 119) the central focus of this chapter is the individual teacher, both in terms of career aspirations and career-oriented actions. Did the teachers in this book have satisfying careers?

The starting point for the analysis is Sikes et al.'s (1985) conclusion that 'teachers differ in their commitment to subject, teaching and school' (p. 192). Looking back at the teachers' stories in this book, such differences are clearly evident. The interesting point is *how* the teachers differed, and why. Commitment ranges from Laura's overbearing enthusiasm for her work and profession, 'it's a vocation ... it's in-built in you, and you've either got it or you haven't'; to Maggie and Grant's focus on subject-based

123

teaching issues; to Edgar's decision to resign from Enterprise High after his 'baptism of fire'; and Jane's decision to escape to the further education sector. Arnold, on the other hand, stayed in post, but without much hope or ambition; while Pete was similarly disillusioned, and also stayed in post, but retained a stubborn belief that his time would come again. Meanwhile, he developed an alternative career interest, a 'side-bet' (Becker, 1960) in the private nursing home industry. If nothing else, these teachers and their stories seem to caution against simplistic generalizations!

Accepting the notions of 'difference' and individuality' in career commitment, as evidenced by the teachers' stories, we felt that it would be helpful to understand more about their individual backgrounds and about the influences upon their career progression. We needed, therefore, to determine the teachers' roots in, and pathways to-date through, the physical education profession. To discover what it means to have a career as a physical education teacher, we wanted to know, both personally and professionally, where the teachers had come from, how far they had come, whether progress matched expectation, and what their future hopes were. In effect, we wanted to examine the 'critical incidents' (Measor, 1985) in the case-study teachers' careers, and how in turn such incidents had shaped their respective careers and identities (Burgess, 1988). The chapter is, therefore, organized into three analytical stages. The first stage, 'Moving in', is concerned with influences which resulted in entry to the physical education profession. The second stage, 'Moving along', is concerned with pressures faced once the goal of being a physical education teacher is achieved. The third stage, 'Moving out', examines the career aspirations of the teachers and their thoughts on promotion which, inevitably it seems, takes them further and further from their sporting roots. So, the first question to ask in investigating their complex career terrain is; what made these teachers become physical educators in the first place?

Moving In: On Becoming a Physical Education Teacher

I said all the time that I was not going to teach, and the only way (my parents could) persuade me to go to college was to say 'if all you want to do is to play sport, well just go and play sport for three years and then maybe we can decide what you want to do'. Maybe because he (dad) could see that I hadn't (laughs) got ability in a lot of other things, he just let me follow what I could do and then sort it out. (Jane)

(I went to college) as an enjoyable way to spend three or four years — to be involved in sport in that way. (Arnold)

We were having our PE. I was standing by the trampoline talking to some boy. He wanted to go [to a local teacher training college] and I thought, 'Oh yes, that's quite good' and, uhm, I like children, and I wanted to keep up my sport and I discussed it with my parents, and we came up with that. (Diane)

All I ever wanted to do was to play sport. (College) was good because we were doing sport pretty much all day every day, which was really what I absolutely loved, y'know. (Grant)

Being a PE teacher is all I ever wanted to be. I get on really well with people generally . . . I also enjoyed sport, and I got so much out of it, socially and physically, I got an awful lot out of it. It was how can I combine these two of my greatest strengths, and I found the ideal place for me. (Laura)

Sport was, invariably, a significant factor in the decisions of the case-study teachers to enter the physical education profession. It is one of the few threads that unites them all and their reasoning appears to be consistent with other physical education teachers and coaches (Dowling Naess,1996; Armour,1997; Templin et al., 1994; Stroot et al., 1994). Perhaps this is unsurprising, as it is logical to assume that entry into most physical activity-related professions would begin with a youthful interest in, and enthusiasm for, sport. Another thread which unites many of the teachers is the influence of their own physical education teachers. The relationships they established, and the consequent images they constructed of these role models were clearly implicated in career choice. Again, this concurs with previous findings (Templin et al., 1994; Stroot et al., 1994). Moreover, as was noted in the previous chapter, these role models are described with great affection, tinged with a sense of awe, with several respondents openly admitting that their teachers influenced them, both in selecting physical education as a career and in choice of training institution. Consequently, some even attended the same higher education institutions as their role-models. As Jane pointed out: 'There was a tradition in the school that all PE teachers came from X college.' This, then, is a powerful factor in the process of 'moving in' to the physical education profession. However, unlike interest in sport, this is only a partial thread. In the case of Laura, for example, physical education teachers are remembered for their appalling, uncaring practice; and for Pete, no-one could match the inspiration provided by his brother — which leads to another clear influence. Six of the eight teachers cited a strong sporting family background as instrumental in cultivating their own love of sport. Notwithstanding that, it is also important to remember that two of the teachers, Arnold and Edgar, had absolutely no family reinforcement at all. So, here again, a thread is evident, but it is only partial. In Edgar's case, it is difficult to see what really motivated his entry into the teaching profession, unless it was just his sheer love of sport. He seems to have fallen in to teaching, almost by chance.

The decision to teach had already been taken by six of the eight case-study teachers as they entered higher education. Jane and Arnold, however, were more interested in playing sport and having a good time. Nevertheless, the college experiences of all the case-study teachers are recalled with longing and fondness, with few reservations: Pete was somewhat regretful that he was rather too old to be at his sporting peak, and Edgar found the academic work demanding. Other than that, the college experience must have been quite something: 'Best three years of my life' (Jane); 'good times (Pete); 'Brilliant, brilliant' (Diane); 'I had the time of my life' (Laura); 'It was good because we were doing sport pretty much all day every day which was really what I absolutely loved' (Grant). It can be speculated that something so good must have been influential — possibly still is. As Bell (1986) notes: 'the expectations which PE teachers have been led to have of themselves through their professional training cannot be discounted' (p. 102). Exactly how that influence is exerted is less certain. As Stroot et al. (1994) conclude after reviewing the available literature: 'We know little about the influence of teacher education in physical education' (p. 345).

These teachers' stories seem to suggest that although active participation in sport did play a role for some in their enjoyment of higher education, of far greater significance was the social life which accompanied sporting involvement. As Diane commented: 'you learn so much about yourself, about other people'; and Grant: 'it was so much freedom, whatever you decide you can do, got to be responsible for every thing you do'. The academic courses undertaken are recalled with mixed feelings, as something to be endured; to be 'slugged through' (Jane); or as an irrelevance, 'I can't really remember anything about them' (Grant). On the other hand, some of the practical lecturers were given a high billing. Certainly none of the academic courses were recalled as vividly or excitedly as the social antics following sports matches! Only Maggie seemed to relish studying for its own sake and, fittingly perhaps, she was the only one to emerge with a first class honours degree. For most of the others, it seems that the sporting environment provided a context for student teachers to establish and develop strong bonds of friendship. Perhaps it was a relief to be surrounded by like-minded people. And perhaps this, in turn, persuaded these teachers of the extrinsic benefits of sport, more so as age and increasing maturity made it all too clear that personal sporting excellence was merely a dream.

Doolittle, Dodds and Placek (1993) found that teacher preparation programmes had little influence on changing the beliefs of pre-service teachers, yet some of these teachers appear to have been, temporarily at least, persuaded by the ideas they encountered. Maggie comments: 'although at college I was very keen on the games for understanding approach . . . I find that sometimes I do have to go back to this business of basics'; and Laura: 'I was personally a great advocate of mixed ability and mixed gender teaching . . . it was the bible . . . I actually now feel that . . . my whole philosophy is changing.' Only now, in the light of experience, are they able to reject those ideas, and the guilt still shows. So teacher education did have an influence — but whether it was positive or not is an interesting debate. Without it, these teachers would have been more akin to Dowling Naess' (1996) case-study teacher, Sven, who developed his physical education teaching from 'a firm foundation of personal physical mastery . . . that gave meaning to his life' (p. 48). On the other hand, for some, particularly Pete, that is exactly what he has done, so the values of his teacher education must have largely passed him by. Here again, the differences between these individual teachers cautions against simple generalizations.

To summarize, the teachers began their journeys into physical education from a firm sporting base. Sport continued in a pivotal role as they embarked upon their teacher training experiences. Somewhere thereafter, its centrality fades as, once employed, teachers encounter the status wall and suddenly find the need to justify their subject and themselves in more acceptable educational/academic terms. Career progression almost certainly depends upon it.

Moving Along: On Being a Physical Education Teacher

Once embarked upon a career in teaching 'many teachers become locked into the system since to leave would require a major disinvestment' (Moreira et al., 1995, p. 123). Such a concept is echoed by Sikes et al. (1985) and Woods (1990) who view mid-career teachers in particular as more prone to becoming entrenched or stuck in the profession. Does this apply to the teachers in this study and, if so, why?

> I don't think that I actually ever get fed up with the teaching itself. Sometimes I think 'this isn't as good as it should be' or, you know 'better work to improve this next time' but it's not the teaching, and I definitely go through phases, especially in the last couple of years that all this new jargon and administration is really too much and is really not for me . . . that makes me fed up. (Jane)

> You get to a point when you just feel 'why bother?' You think 'there must be something better than this.' I quite often get miserable or depressed . . . fed up with the teaching situation. The whole problem with teaching is

everything is attached to your teaching subject. If I could just have a pastoral role, that would be OK. (Arnold)

I want everyone to achieve. I don't ever want that (loss of enthusiasm) to happen to me. The minute that starts happening to me in teaching, I'm getting out or I'm getting into another area of the job. When I've lost my enthusiasm and dedication, then that'll happen. (Laura)

A situation's been created here where I'm gonna stay at Citylimits as long as I want to. Citylimits will not give me the mental kick that my other life gives me outside, 'cos my outside life, I am in full control of and that will stimulate me. I am in full control of that. (Pete)

The teachers' comments seem to reinforce Moreira et al.'s (1995) premise that 'commitment is not a uniform commodity, but rather something that ebbs and flows depending upon changes in the task (job), career and extramural domains' of life (p. 124). Pete's 'extramural domain', as was noted earlier, centred on a private nursing home venture he ran with his wife. However, even though this gives him the economic independence to leave teaching, he chooses not to. His 'side-bet' (Becker, 1960) could well be the result of his general dissatisfaction with a school system he believes is failing pupils (Sikes et al., 1985) but perhaps his investment in his career has been too substantial to simply leave. While his enthusiasm to teach sport within the curriculum remains high, he is likely to stay. In contrast to Pete, Arnold's 'side-bet' has been his growing involvement in pastoral care, thus increasing his investment in a career structure to which he has never been fully committed: 'Yeah all the way through, right from when I started, there's always been an eye on the look out for something else.' Indeed, Arnold appears the least subject-committed of the teachers, while simultaneously, and almost perversely, being highly regarded by other staff and the senior management team at Citylimits. Perhaps as long as one is well versed in educational jargon, one's stock as a physical educator can remain high. Yet again, the applicability of Sparkes' (1987) concept of 'strategic rhetoric' is confirmed. However, Arnold is trapped. He is aware of the marginal nature of his subject and, thus, has devoted an increasing amount of time to pastoral issues in an attempt to develop an alternative career structure for himself. Currently Arnold appears to be pursuing a career in teaching because he can envisage no realistic alternatives (Moreira et al., 1995): he is negatively motivated to stay, and it's beginning to show.

The despondency characterised by Arnold was not representative of other teachers in this study. Laura, Grant, Maggie and Diane all demonstrated great enthusiasm and motivation for their work; much of which was expressed in a multi-faceted caring philosophy for the pupils. Jane, on a declining continuum of enthusiasm, appeared a little more weary (due in no small part to her daily dose of skirmishing with Pete), but managed to rekindle her interest with a move to a college of further education. She is still 'investing'. Indeed, even Edgar, whose disillusionment led him to resign his post at Enterprise High, was back teaching almost immediately, lending support to Cole's (1985) findings that even disaffected students were prepared to embark on a teaching career due to perceptions about the magnitude of the investment already made. Once in, teachers certainly seem to find it difficult to get out.

Diane also appears to be 'investing' time and energy outside physical education, although her reasons are a little different to those of Pete and Arnold. Diane fully intends to 'construct' a career of her own design. Therefore, she decided that the time had come for some promotion and, to that end, she applied for, and was awarded, an incentive allowance relating to managing the school minibus. Although she would have preferred an allowance for physical education, this was not going to become available and, as she put it, 'I felt I had to get on an incentive this year, some way or another. I wouldn't have been happy staying on the main grade for another year'. Even administrator of the school minibus, it seems, was more highly regarded than being a good teacher of physical education at Citylimits High School. In addition to the financial motive, Diane also believes that involving herself in broader school initiatives will give her greater visibility within the school hierarchy. It is likely, of course, that Diane's double-edged investment serves to lock her ever tighter into her career, as to leave now would certainly require a major disinvestment on her part. However, with the optimism of youth, she does not foresee any problems.

The younger teachers (Diane, Maggie, Laura, Grant) certainly gave the impression that they remain in teaching because they genuinely love the job. As Maggie comments: 'everyday [with the pupils] something positive happens'. In comparison, Pete and Arnold, appear to possess relatively weak teacher identities (Dowling Naess, 1996), but for differing reasons. Arnold's stems from his fragile commitment to the profession in general: 'I'm on the look out for some thing else, something more glamorous, attractive, with more money and less hassle.' Pete's weak teacher identity on the other hand, emanates from the fact that he really doesn't need the salary: his 'side-bet' has made him financially independent, and also because of his studied and visible identification with sport which he knows is an irritation to colleagues and senior managers. Thus, similar to Dowling Naess' (1996) respondent, Sven Hoel, sport has provided his identity within the profession with focus, form and substance. Moreover, in connecting his personal experience of physical activity to his teaching, Pete's philosophy allows little room for reflection on deeply held beliefs and, in turn, represents a celebration of a traditional vision of masculinity (George and Kirk, 1988). Not that this is necessarily a problem, but it does present difficulties for colleagues who are trying to challenge the macho stereotype which has bedevilled physical education and its teachers. Dowling Naess' (1996) seems to capture Pete in a nutshell: 'In Lawson's terms he has been socialised via sport with all its attendant problems of a tendency towards conservatism, convention and the reproduction of given experiences' (p. 49). Socialization via sport may well bring with it problematic baggage, but Pete is still positively motivated to stay in teaching, which is more than can be said for Arnold. Indeed, Arnold appears dissatisfied with all aspects of the profession; a disaffection illustrated in his gloomy prediction that 'Diane's early drive and enthusiasm is due to the fact that she is early into the system . . . she'll inevitably become worn out or beaten by the system'. We have to hope that his prophecy is as misplaced as is his current role in teaching physical education. Time will tell.

Moving Out

As teachers progress up and through their careers, they are increasingly faced with decisions which could effectively relocate them in administrative roles, as opposed to teaching roles (Moreira et al., 1995). This proves a major dilemma for many, who naturally seek advancement in their chosen profession, but at the price of increasingly divorcing themselves from the pupils and, more particularly, their subject. The teachers in this book illustrate the conundrum well. Laura, in particular, was hesitant about 'moving up' in the school hierarchy, as this invariably involved 'moving out' of sport and the valued environment where she mixes with pupils:

> I'm aware that I've achieved a lot very quickly, and I give a lot to my subject, but the higher up you go, the more distanced you get from the children. The higher up you get, it becomes a 'them' and 'us'. It's in the future though. (Laura)

Similarly, and as was noted in Chapter 12, Jane despaired at the administration that accompanied her head of department post: 'The main things that get me fed up with teaching are . . . the administration . . . I just can't get along with all this admin.' Administration for Jane appears to cover various initiatives and responsibilities that take her away from contact with the pupils in her subject; a much preferred use of her time. That much of this administration stems from outside her department is of even greater irritation to her. Consequently, she had no wish to progress any higher up the hierarchy of school management as this would simply exacerbate the situation. Such findings concur with the work of Schempp (1993), whose research subject, Steve Sommers, 'when discussing career aspirations said that he would not want to be a principal because "having to justify every roll of toilet paper I buy and having my policies questioned every minute" was not something he cared to tolerate' (p. 8). Edgar's story echoes a similar sentiment. The increased administrative workload, and the responsibility, which accompanied his temporary promotion to acting head of department at Enterprise High were instrumental in his decision to resign. As an inexperienced teacher, he was overwhelmed by the pressures of the changing nature of his work and strained relations with departmental colleagues.

Arnold, as ever, is rather different. He was one of only two teachers in this study who entered higher education without a firm intention to be a teacher. In sharp contrast to all the other teachers, he has no desire to remain within, or even linked to, physical education, and is actively trying to forge a career elsewhere in the school. If he could, he would leave the subject behind, as he commented: 'The whole problem with teaching, is that everything is attached to your teaching subject.' So, whereas the other teachers expressed a desire to maintain contact with their subject base as they 'move up' through their careers, Arnold desperately wants to divorce himself from it; he wants to move out. Unfortunately, as was noted earlier, he has not found satisfaction in the pastoral route either and his pathway to fulfilment and satisfaction within education still resembles more of a quagmire than a motorway.

Thus, the career paradox emerges. Physical education teachers are in a no-win situation, which perhaps goes some way to explain their numerical absence from school senior management positions. The subject-committed teachers are reluctant to leave their roots, yet they find it almost impossible, if they are to progress, to retain links with a subject base that has little status and value in the educational context (see previous chapter). On the other hand, if they promote the idea that physical education teachers have a unique role in the social and moral education of pupils, and then select the obvious pastoral route to promotion, they merely serve to emphasize still further that they are unlike other mainstream subject staff who have a much wider range of promotion routes open to *them*. It seems extraordinarily difficult for physical education teachers to 'move along', and then 'move up' in a smooth career pathway, and it seems extraordinarily limiting to suggest that they must 'move out' of physical education if they are to forge ahead. Such obstacles to advancement for physical education teachers have long been identified (Sparkes and Templin, 1992; Ball, 1987).

The careers of individual teachers are undoubtedly partially structured by the workplace ideology (Evans and Williams, 1989), which includes an institutionalized pattern of disadvantage for physical education teachers centring on the subject's lack of academic status. Thus, as Evans and Williams (1989) confirm, advancement through teaching is unequal, due to the varying status and professional resources possessed by different teachers and their subjects: 'Apparently, those who choose to teach the more practical subjects are unable to compete with other subjects and are (therefore) destined to remain on the lower rungs of the managerial ladder' (Sparkes and Templin, 1992, p. 131). How others in a school perceive a curriculum subject clearly has a material influence over those who teach that subject and, as was noted in the last chapter, the role of the wider education profession in perpetuating status difficulties for physical education might bear some scrutiny.

The stories by teachers in this book suggest that investments made by the more committed individuals were repaid in intrinsic rewards, such as interaction with pupils and seeing those pupils learn and experience success in physical activities. These teachers were, as might be expected, also the most concerned that advancement in the profession would cut into their time to achieve such rewards, thus the nature of the investment would have to evolve from intrinsic to extrinsic. All of the case-study teachers felt they had invested heavily in numerous ways in their careers, therefore to leave would require a major disinvestment on their behalf; a step they are naturally reluctant to take. Some do indeed appear to be 'locked' into a profession which is perceived as constraining, but which requires more and more investment. Nevertheless, despite the apparent contextual constraints, many of the case-study teachers, with the obvious exception of Arnold and to a lesser extent Pete, were forging satisfying careers for themselves as physical educators. Pete and Arnold most closely resemble Templin's (1989) subject Sarah who was 'running on ice', in that they felt constrained in their attempts to develop a meaningful physical education programme for themselves and their students. However, most of the other teachers seemed to be successfully negotiating their careers in teaching 'relative to personal and professional goals'(Templin et al., 1994, p. 275). The shame is that such positions have invariably been reached very much in spite of, not because of, the system.

And so the vicious circle endures — those physical education teachers who do achieve career progression have little visible connection to those who are seeking to progress, because to progress is to leave physical education behind. Thus, it is, that we can identify a thread running through all the 'theme chapters': from the difficulties emanating from the practical nature of physical education and its close relationship to sport, which were analyzed in Chapter 10; to the overwhelming and enduring status concerns highlighted in Chapter 11; to the problems inherent in implicating physical education in a unique role in pupils' social and moral education in Chapter 12; and, finally, to what now appears to be the inevitable outcome — poor career opportunities within secondary schools. Although a gloomy note upon which to end, it is tempting to wonder whether the whole process is so entrenched and enmeshed as to be completely impenetrable.

Yet, to despair at this stage is to be self-indulgent. The three earlier theme chapters pointed to a need for fundamental research in physical education and it seems certain that this is the key to the problem. Until we, in the physical education profession, have more research-based knowledge about the educational value of physical education, we will be unable to start unravelling the web which entangles physical education teachers and their careers. There is no short cut, and perhaps the remaining task of this book is to identify more clearly what that research process might entail.

Chapter 14

Physical Education, Sport and Educational Status: The Case for Fundamental Research

This is not an easy book to conclude. The teachers' lives go on, so there is no meaningful way in which their stories can be concluded. Rather, it is tempting to resume the interview process, just to see how the teachers' philosophies and careers continue to evolve. But then the book would never be finished. So, instead, conclusions are drawn from the analytical theme chapters which, in turn, are underpinned by the teachers' stories. Concluding comments are grouped into five sections representing the threads which run through all the chapters in the book.

Status

The issue of status reverberates throughout this book. It is an intractable problem for physical education and a key characteristic of the lives and careers of physical education teachers. In Chapter 10, the complex relationship between physical education and sport was explored in various contexts: in the context of the teachers' stories; in critical analysis of the title 'physical education'; in a consideration of dualism in education; and in the light of the low status of practical knowledge. In the course of the discussion, a question was raised: 'Why seek to make a distinction between physical education and sport?' The analysis which followed pointed to the inescapable conclusion that neither sport nor physical education are viewed as educationally worthy — at least in the high-status academic sense. Furthermore, in the populist split between mind and body, physical education — even by its very name — is firmly linked to the low-status body. To compound the matter further, physical education teachers are often to be seen teaching sports to pupils, undermining their claims to be doing something qualitatively different. In Chapter 11, the status issue was further pursued at three levels: 'Us', examining ways in which we, in the physical education profession, create and sustain the status difficulties we face; 'Them', in the broader education community, looking at ways in which colleagues may be culpable in the maintenance of status problems; and, finally, 'We', focusing on the need for educators to work together to remedy the status crisis in physical education. Emerging from both chapters is a plea for the profession to undertake fundamental research into the educational value of physical education and, in particular, into one of its core — and highly visible components — sport.

In Chapter 11, two 'status-solutions' which emerged from the teachers' stories were also considered. Health/fitness knowledge claims for physical education, although widely espoused and generally endorsed, were difficult to substantiate. The imperative to be realistic about such claims was thus indicated. As Kirk (1988) suggests: 'what is required . . . is a degree of moderation in using the health focus to delimit the programme' (p. 155). The second 'status-solution' offered was the advent of examination courses in physical education. However, it was the theoretical content of those courses, and the fact that they were examined in traditional fashion, which teachers viewed as status-enhancing. This led to questions about the wisdom of vesting status hopes in theory, when the subject matter of physical education is largely practical. Kirk (1988) puts it bluntly: 'In terms of physical education becoming an acceptable "academic" subject, this is unlikely to happen for the simple reason that the subject is based in physical activity' (p. 151).

Chapter 12 continued the status theme. In what might be viewed as a third 'status-solution', teachers in this book also implied that they, as physical education teachers, have a special role in pupils' social and moral education. This claim appeared to have three interrelated dimensions: the physical education teacher as a unique caring individual; the social and moral values inherent in the subject matter, particularly sport; and the teacher as influential role-model in the relatively informal environment that characterizes physical education lessons. Once again, it was difficult to substantiate some of these claims, although teachers clearly felt that the three dimensions of caring were 'natural' and important components of their roles as physical education professionals. Miller, Bredmeier and Shields (1997) would agree with them: 'physical education is a rich context for promoting sociomoral development' (p. 49). In an ironic twist, however, none of the teachers cited pupils' social/moral development as the 'high point' of teaching. Rather they focused, albeit apologetically, on seeing pupils acquire and improve physical skills in a sporting context. That they were apologetic, seems to speak volumes about the value which attaches to physical and sporting achievements in the educational community.

In Chapter 13, career progression in physical education was examined and the status threads seemed to converge. Teachers' careers were examined in three stages: moving into the profession; moving along a career pathway;

and, finally, moving out of physical education in the interests of gaining promotion. An invidious career paradox emerged from the analysis. It would appear that, more than most teachers, physical education teachers may be forced to choose between promotion and their teaching subject. In so doing, those who are promoted are visibly distanced from physical education, implying that promotion and physical education are incompatible. Furthermore, those seeking promotion tend to follow the limited pastoral route, intensifying the claim that, by virtue of their subject matter, they have had a unique role in pupils' social and moral education. Teachers of other subjects are not so self-limiting in their career avenues. As was noted at the end of the chapter, the status issue threads through all the theme chapters, the outcome of which is the relatively poor career outlook of many physical education teachers. So, given that attempts by the physical education profession to claim status have had little effect to date, what is to be done?

Looking Back to See Ahead

Perhaps the most sobering feature of this research process has been the degree of insight found in historical literature on physical education from the 1960s and 1970s. We might hope that each generation learns from the last, and that knowledge in physical education would continuously build and improve much as it does, for example, in medical research. After all, the education of young people is an important enterprise. However, Paul (1996) notes Eleanor Metheney's observation from 1970 that 'each new generation of leaders in the field thinks they know more about physical education than did their ancestors'. Combine that with Paul's charge that 'we have always had conflicting ideas of purpose' (p. 541) and it explains why we have made limited progress in raising the status of physical education in schools. If we are not drawing upon wisdom from the past then we are, in effect, constantly reinventing a slightly wobbly wheel. This seems rather wasteful, as a glance at some of the work of earlier writers demonstrates. It becomes apparent, for example, that some had advice which we might usefully have heeded. Consider the following from the conclusion of a book entitled *Education and Physical Education*:

> Children grow and develop, not only physically, but also mentally and emotionally. Teachers of physical education are clearly concerned with physical growth and development, but need to decide not only how much they are implicated or involved with the all-round development of children, *but also how best they can indicate this involvement, how much they can do to justify it, and how important they think it is. Too many wild claims have been made in the past about the general effects of physical*

education, these claims often being on the side of emotional development. No assertions about the effects of any of the branches of physical education should be made which cannot be substantiated. Opinions may be held about these effects, but these should be put forward honestly as opinions, until they have been submitted to the test of investigation. (Myrle James, 1967, pp. 77–8, our emphasis)

Based on the evidence presented in this book, these would seem to be wise words indeed. We might conclude that physical educationists are long on opinion and rather short on substantiated claims about the educational value of their subject. In a fascinating parallel, Kirk (1997) recently seems to have echoed Myrle James' caution in the context of introducing change in physical education:

It is my firm conviction that educational research should lead educational reform and that our advocacies for change should be well-grounded, well-informed, and we can say as best as we are able what outcomes the proposed programs might produce. (p. 185)

It is an important point which, in the opinion of the authors, cannot be overstated. Without a research-supported foundation, physical educationists flounder when they need to articulate their worth in the school context, as was demonstrated by the internal tensions evident in the teachers' interview comments in this book. Fernandez-Balboa (1997) suggests that 'despite their strong interest in sport, movement and education, many physical educators lack a relational understanding of the complex, intersecting connections among physical activity, the school, culture, and society' (p. 162). The implication is that, by gaining such understanding, physical educators will be able to address the status difficulties which their subject faces in schools. That is undoubtedly true — in part. However, what is being suggested here is that there is something even more fundamental missing.

'Fundamental Research' in Physical Education

As was noted at the end of the previous chapter, the remaining task of this book is to identify what *fundamental* research in physical education would look like. What do we need to know about physical education that we do not already know? Arnold (1968) made one suggestion:

Physical education is a subject and yet more than a subject. It is to do with skills, yet perhaps more important it is to do with the person. With its multifarious activities and possibilities it covers everything in education which is to do with the physical ... For physical education teachers, whose minds are preoccupied by method and function, the reason *why* they are doing what they are doing must remain a puzzle. Their uncertainty of thought is ruthlessly exposed by their pupils who ask why it is they have to 'waste time' with PE ... To be able to give satisfactory answers to questions of this sort it is necessary for the teacher of physical education to have a *raison d'etre* which is based upon a thought-out position of educational philosophy. Hackneyed phrases and clichés are not enough. They are often a cover for superficial and ill-equipped minds which are used but which lack direction and purpose. (p. 8)

From Arnold (1968) then, over 30 years ago, it was a clear educational philosophy which was required. Reid (1997) would argue that it is *still* required and he proposes a philosophy based on 'Value Pluralism' in response to the 'incorrigibly marginal status' (p. 6) of physical education. However, if Paul's (1996) historical analysis, noted earlier, is accepted, it would appear that we have had a surfeit of value pluralism in physical education, and it has not served us well. Reid (1997) argues that 'a pluralistic account of value is required to capture the variety of ways in which physical educa-tion satisfies the value condition of education' (p. 17). Perhaps so, and this approach would seem to have potential at some stage, but maybe Reid's quest is premature. There is a requirement for something even more funda-mental which precedes a philosophical account of value. Arnold (1968) claimed that 'The PE teacher ... alone is concerned with his (sic) pupils' bodies as well as their intellect, emotions and sociability, and because of this he has enormous educative scope' (p. 9). That, in a nutshell, is the fundamental research that is required. We need to know more about that 'enormous educative scope' in the context of the practical activities that constitute much of the physical education curriculum. And we need to *know* specifics, rather than express opinions, hopes or intentions. In short we need to follow the historical advice of Myrle James (1967) and the current advice of Kirk (1997) — do the research first. So, how to proceed?

The only way forward that we, the authors, can envisage is painstak-ing and detailed research which observes teaching and learning in practical physical education; which discusses such teaching and learning with the participants (teachers and pupils); and which verifies knowledge claims thus identified in national and international contexts. Following this, a Great Debate in physical education should be initiated, the outcome of which ought to be some broad agreement about the actuality of our educational potential. It would appear that we have attempted to run before we can walk — rather a silly error for physical educationists. Whereas we have detailed research on a whole range of issues in physical education, we have yet to do the ground-work which would enable us to claim our rightful place at the heart of the education process. Rather, *we* are convinced of our value, but we are expecting too much of others simply to take our word for it: evidence speaks louder. In similar vein, Hargreaves (1982) advises that:

> If PE is to improve its status as a school subject, PE teachers will have to be prepared to fight for it. Nobody else is going to grant such a status ... (and) the PE teacher must realise that this entails arguing that PE is more important than some other subjects. (p. 9)

Kirk's (1988) response is to exhort teachers to 'political action ... but first we have to believe in ourselves and the worth of our subject' (p. 161). The suggestion we are making in this book is that there is no short cut to status. We need to return to the central activities of physical education, the practical activities, and we need to understand more about their educative value if we are to 'believe in ourselves'. Moreover, given that many of those practical activities are sports, we have to recognize that the interrelationship between physical education and sport will continue to be a significant factor in our deliberations.

Sport

Like others in the profession, we wonder whether the time has come to call a truce between physical education and sport. Like it or not, physical education teachers are closely identified with sport. As the evidence in this and other research shows, teachers have both personal and professional links to sport and they enjoy the intrinsic rewards that pupils' sporting achievements can bring. And why not? Maybe physical educationists ought to trust their instincts — perhaps sport does, after all, offer unique opportunities for learning. But, as has been argued above, those hunches must be substantiated. If links to sport are inevitable, then surely the way forward is to provide *proof* — research-based proof — of the broad educational potential of sporting activities. It should be stressed that this is a different approach to those who advocate Sport Education (Seidentop, 1987). We would view Sport Education as unnecessarily limiting. Instead, we see educational possibilities in sport which transcend the rather narrow sport-focus of Sport Education. We would not, for example, place sport at the heart of the educational process, rather we see the child at the centre and sport as the ultimate tool for educating 'the whole child'. In this respect, we are matched by no other curriculum subject. As Hargreaves (1982) pointed out earlier, these are the type of self-interested arguments that we must be willing to advance.

Sharp's (1994) description of football (soccer) might provide a way forward. In a bold and entirely unashamed statement to a broad academic audience, he made a startling claim about football: 'This is physical chess. It is chess played fast.' Described in those terms football, and by implication other team sports, take on a whole new meaning in an educational context. It is an exciting thought and if it can be substantiated by empirical evidence, then it lends greater weight to those researchers who argue for equity for pupils in the provision of curricular and extra-curricular sporting activities (Penney and Harris, 1997). No pupil should be denied the challenging educational experience of physical chess! But what of the teachers of 'physical chess'; what would they look like?

Critical, Confident, Thinking Physical Education Teachers

Finally, and fittingly, the discussion returns to where it all started — teachers themselves. Sport played a major role in the lives and careers of the physical education teachers in this book. Evidence from national and international research made it clear that they are not unusual in that respect. However, for the reasons outlined in earlier chapters, links to sport are largely unhelpful in educational terms, although sport may be valued in schools for its marketing potential. Clearly that's not enough. So, how can we help more physical education teachers to feel valued, and be valued?

Physical educators are often described, usually disparagingly, as 'traditional' in their outlook:

> In general, physical educators are quite conservative and the causes for this may be traced to their professional and occupational socialisation. (Lawson, 1988). Physical educators are attracted to, and socialized by, two traditionally conservative social institutions (i.e., schooling and sport) and hence their attitudes and actions are more aimed at reproducing the dominant curricular orientations than at transforming them. (Fernandez-Balboa, 1997, p. 162)

However, there is another important point to be made about physical educators, and it is the key to understanding their actions. Throughout schooling, and even during higher education, they have encountered indifference, or even hostility, towards their interest and achievement in sport (see Kretchmar, 1996). They will be in no doubt, therefore, about the low status of themselves, of sport and of physical skills in education. Unsurprisingly, some of them become defensive, reluctant to challenge sporting practices and traditions — even where they are blatantly inequitable — and, occasionally, arrogant. Can we really blame them? Kirk (1997) suggests that:

... physical educators must develop skills that permit us to be leaders rather than followers of social change, to be proactive shapers of the future rather than reactors to others' initiatives. In short, we must develop the collective capacity to think beyond the square — to imagine possibilities and alternatives that are not bound by convention or by past practice but that instead provides a means of coping most adequately with a plethora of uncertain, hard to predict but possible futures. (p. 182)

A tall order for anyone! Yet many physical educators are resilient and resourceful, as has been demonstrated throughout this book. What they lack is security in their educational value. This, then, is the main rationale for undertaking fundamental research in physical education. The profession needs empirical evidence to substantiate knowledge claims for practical activities in physical education. This can provide a firm, confident base upon which teachers can develop into thinking, critical professionals. Conversely, time spent feeling defensive and undervalued is both wearing and distracting, as some of the teachers' stories showed. The role of teacher education then becomes clearer. Its task is to ensure that students are fully cogniscent with the research evidence and are acutely aware of the unique educational potential of their subject. Moreover, as talented and enthusiastic sports performers themselves, many of them can begin to enjoy a certain educational pride in the nature of their achievements. Indeed, if sports are 'physical chess', then physical educators ought to consider themselves to be Grand Masters (and Grand Dames), with the awesome responsibility of enthusing and enabling young people to reach for the level of their own capabilities. Now *that* is a career worth having.

References

ALMOND, L., HARRISON, P. and LAWS, C. (1996) 'Sport — raising the game: A P.E. perspective', *The British Journal of Physical Education*, **27**, 3, pp. 6–11.

APPLEYARD, B. (1991) 'The revolution that turned education sentimental', *The Sunday Times*, 28 April.

ARMOUR, K.M. (1993) 'The ecology of physical education: An investigation into the 'life' of a physical education department and its impact upon the identities and opportunities of pupils and teachers', Unpublished PhD Thesis, University of Southampton.

ARMOUR, K.M. (1996) 'The successful physical education department: Personal perspectives of the senior management team in a secondary school', *The British Journal of Physical Education*, **27**, 4, pp. 25–7.

ARMOUR, K.M. (1997) 'Developing a personal philosophy on the nature and purpose of physical education: Life history reflections', *European Physical Education Review*, **3**, 1, pp. 68–82.

ARNOLD, P.J. (1968) *Education, Physical Education and Personality Development*, London: Heinemann.

ARNOLD, P.J. (1984) 'Sport, moral education and the development of character', *Journal of Philosophy of Education*, 18, pp. 275–81.

ARNOLD, P.J. (1985) 'Rational planning by objectives of the movement curriculum', *Physical Education Review*, **8**, 1, pp. 50–61.

ARNOLD, P.J. (1996) 'Olympism, sport and education', *Quest*, 48, pp. 93–101.

ARNOLD, P.J. (1997) *Sport, Ethics and Education,* London: Cassell.

BALL, S. (1987) *The Micro-Politics of the School*, London: Meuthen.

BALL, S. and GOODSON, I. (1985) 'Understanding teachers: Concepts and contexts', in BALL, S. and GOODSON, I. (eds), *Teachers Lives and Careers*, London: Falmer Press, pp. 1–26.

BECK, M. (1990) 'Physical education is more than sport', *British Journal of Physical Education*, **21**, 3, p. 356.

BECKER, H.S. (1960) 'Notes on the concept of commitment', *American Journal of Sociology*, 66, pp. 32–40.

BECKER, H.S. (1990) 'Generalizing from case studies', in EISNER, E.W. and PESHKIN, A. (eds) *Qualitative Research in Education: The Continuing Debate*, New York: Teachers College Press, pp. 233–42.

BELL, L.A. (1986) 'Managing to survive in a secondary school', in EVANS, J. (ed.) *Physical Education Sport and Schooling: Studies in the Sociology of Physical Education*, London: Falmer Press, pp. 95–116.

BROOKER, R. and MACDONALD, D. (1995) 'Mapping physical education in the reform agenda for Australian education: Tensions and contradictions', *European Physical Education Review*, **1**, 2, pp. 101–10.

BUBER, M. (1970) *I and Thou* (Trans Walter Kaufman), New York: Charles Scriber's Sons.

BURGESS, R.G. (1988) 'Promotion and the physical education teacher', in EVANS, J. (ed.) *Teachers, Teaching and Control in Physical Education*, London: Falmer Press, pp. 41–56.

CARLISLE, R. (1977) 'The concept of excellence in physical education', in GLAISTER, I.K. (ed.) *The Pursuit of Excellence in Sport and Physical Education*, Report of the NATFHE PE Section Conference, College of Ripon and York St. John, York, pp. 19–26.

CARR, D. (1983) 'On physical education and educational significance', *Momentum*, **8**, 3, pp. 2–9.

CHELLADURAI, P. and KUGA, D.J. (1996) 'Teaching and coaching: Group and task differences', *Quest*, **48**, 4, pp. 470–85.

COLE, M. (1985) 'The tender trap? Commitment and consciousness in entrants to teaching', in BALL, S. and GOODSON, I. (eds) *Teachers Lives and Careers*, London: Falmer Press, pp. 89–104.

COLQUHOUN, D. (1989) 'H.R.F. and individualism: Continuing the debate', *British Journal of Physical Education*, **21**, 2, pp. 231–2.

CONNELL, R.W. (1985) *Teachers' Work*, Sydney, Australia: Allen and Unwin.

CURTNER-SMITH, M.D., KERR, I.G. and CLAPP, A.J. (1996) 'The impact of National Curriculum physical education on the teaching of health-related fitness: A casestudy in one English town', *European Journal of Physical Education*, **1**, 1, pp. 66–83.

DEPARTMENT FOR EDUCATION (DFE)/WELSH OFFICE (WO) (1995) *Physical Education in the National Curriculum*, London: DFE.

DEPARTMENT OF EDUCATION AND SCIENCE (DES) (1952) *Moving and Growing: Physical Education in the Primary School. Part 1*, London: HMSO.

DEPARTMENT OF EDUCATION AND SCIENCE (DES) (1989) *National Curriculum — From policy to practice*, London: DES.

DEPARTMENT OF EDUCATION AND SCIENCE (DES) (1992) *Physical Education in the National Curriculum*, London: HMSO.

DEPARTMENT OF NATIONAL HERITAGE (DNH) (1995) Sport — Raising the Game, London: DNH.

DOOLITTLE, S., DODDS, P. and PLACEK, J.H. (1993) 'Persistence of beliefs about teaching during formal training of pre-service teachers', in STROOT, S. (ed.) Socialization into physical education [Monograph]. *Journal of Teaching in Physical Education*, 12, pp. 355–65.

DOWLING NAESS, F.J. (1996) 'Life events and curriculum change: The life history of a Norwegian Educator', *European Physical Education Review*, **2**, 1, pp. 41–53.

ELBAZ, F. (1991) 'Research on teachers' knowledge: The evolution of a discourse', *Journal of Curriculum Studies*, **23**, 1, pp. 1–19.

EVANS, J. (1989) 'Health related fitness: A suitable case for treatment', *British Journal of Physical Education*, **20**, 4, pp. 189–90.

EVANS, J. (1990b) 'Sport education: Is it physical education by another name?' *The ACHPER National Journal*, March, pp. 12–18.

EVANS, J. and DAVIES, B. (1988) 'Introduction: Teachers, teaching and Control', in EVANS, J. (ed.) *Teachers, Teaching and Control in Physical Education*, London: Falmer Press, pp. 1–20.

EVANS, J., PENNEY, D. and DAVIES, B. (1996) 'Back to the future: Education, policy and physical education', in ARMSTRONG, N. (ed.) *New Directions in Physical Education*, London: Cassell, pp. 1–18.

EVANS, J. and WILLIAMS, T. (1989) 'Moving up and getting out: The classed and gendered career opportunities of physical education teachers', in TEMPLIN, T.J. and SCHEMPP, P. (eds) *Socialization into Physical Education: Learning to Teach*, Indianapoils, IN.: Benchmark, pp. 235–49.

FERNANDEZ-BALBOA, J.M. (1993) 'Sociocultural characteristics of the hidden curriculum in physical education', *Quest*, 45, pp. 230–54.

FERNANDEZ-BALBOA, J.M. (1995) 'Reclaiming physical education in higher education through critical pedagogy', *Quest*, 47, pp. 91–114.

FERNANDEZ-BALBOA, J.M. (1997) 'Knowledge base in physical education: a proposal for a new era', *Quest*, 49, pp. 161–81.

GEERTZ, C. (1973). 'Thick description: Toward an interpretive theory of culture', in GEERTZ, C. (ed.) *The Interpretation of Cultures*, New York: Basic Books, pp. 3–30.

GEERTZ, C. (1988) *Works and Lives: The Anthropologist as Author*, Cambridge: Polity Press.

GEORGE, L. and KIRK, D. (1988) 'The limits of change in physical education: Ideologies, teachers and the experience of physical activity', in EVANS, J. (ed.) *Teachers, Teaching and Control in Physical Education*, London: Falmer Press, pp. 145–56.

GIROUX, H.A. (1991) 'Democracy and the discourse of cultural difference: Towards a politics of border pedagogy', *British Journal of Sociology of Education*, **12**, 4, pp. 501–19.

HAMMERSLEY, M. and ATKINSON, P. (1983) *Ethnography: Principles in Practice*, London: Tavistock.

HARGREAVES, D.H. (1982) 'Ten proposals for the future of physical education', *Bulletin of Physical Education*, **18**, 3, pp. 5–10.

HARRIS, J. and CALE, L. (1997) 'Activity promotion in physical education', *European Physical Education Review*, **3**, 1, pp. 58–67.

HARRISON, B.W. (1985) 'The power and anger in the work of love: Christian ethics for women and other strangers', in ROBB, C.S. (ed.) *Making the Connections: Essays in Feminist Social Ethics*, Boston: Beacon, pp. 3–21.

HER MAJESTY'S INSPECTORATE (HMI) (1989) *Physical Education from 5 to 16. Curriculum Matters 16*, London: HMSO.

HIRST, P.H. (1974) *Knowledge and the Curriculum*, London: RKP.

HOLT, R. (1992) 'Amateurism and its interpretation: The social origins of British sport', *Innovation*, **5**, 4, pp. 19–31.

KEDDIE, N. (1971) 'Classroom knowledge', in YOUNG, M.F.D. (ed.) *Knowledge and Control*, London: Collier Macmillan, pp. 133–60.

KEGAN, R. (1982) *The Evolving Self: Problem and Process in Human Development*, Cambridge, MA.: Harvard University Press.

KIRK, D. (1988) *Physical Education and Curriculum Study: A Critical Introduction*, London: Croon Helm.

KIRK, D. (1994) 'Making the present strange: Sources of the present crisis in physical education', *Discourse*, **15**, 1, pp. 46–53.

KIRK, D. (1997) 'Thinking beyond the square: The challenge to physical educators in new times', *Quest*, 49, pp. 182–6.

KIRK, D. and TINNING, R. (1990*) Physical Education, Curriculum and Culture: Critical Issues in the Contemporary Crisis*, London: Falmer Press.

KRETCHMAR, S. (1996) 'Movement and play on higher education's contested terrain', *Quest*, pp. 433–41.

LAWN, M. and BARTON, L. (eds) (1981) *Rethinking Curriculum Studies*, London, Croon Helm.

LAWSON, H. (1983) 'Toward a model of teacher socialization in physical education: The subjective warrant, recruitment and teacher education', *Journal of Teaching in Physical Education*, **2**, 3, pp. 3–16.

LAWSON, H. (1988) 'Occupational socialization, cultural studies and the physical education curriculum', *Journal of Teaching in Physical Education*, 7, pp. 265–88.

LEE, M. (1996) 'Psycho-social development from 5–16 years', *New Directions in Physical Education: Change and Innovation*, London: Cassell, pp. 33–47.

LOCKE, L. (1987) 'Research and the improvement of teaching: The professor as the problem' in BARETTE, G.T., FEINGOLD, R.S., ROGER REES, C., and PIERON, M. (eds) *Myths, Models and Methods in Sport Pedagogy*, Proceedings of the Adelphi-AIESEP 1985 World Sport Conference, August 19–22, Adelphi University, New York, Champaign, Il.: Human Kinetics Publishers, Inc.

LOCKE, L. (1989) 'Qualitative research as a form of scientific inquiry in sport and physical education', *Research Quarterly in Exercise and Sport*, **60**, pp. 1–20.

MACDONALD, D. (1995) 'The role of proletarianization in physical education teacher attrition', *Research Quarterly for Exercise and Sport Science*, 66, pp. 129–41.

MACDONALD, D. and BROOKER, R. (1995) 'Professional education: Tensions in subject design and implementation', *Education Research and Perspectives*, December, **22**, 2, pp. 99–109.

MACDONALD, D. and BROOKER, R. (1997) 'Moving beyond the crisis in secondary physical education: An Australian initiative', *Journal of Teaching in Physical Education*, 16, pp. 155–75.

MARDLE, G. and WALKER, M. (1980) 'Strategies and structure: Some critical notes on teacher socialization', in WOODS, P. (ed.) *Teacher Strategies*, London: Croon Helm, pp. 98–124.

MAXWELL, J.A. (1992) 'Understanding and validity in qualitative research', *Harvard Educational Review*, **62**, 3, pp. 279–300.

MEAKIN, D.C. (1983) 'On the justification of physical education', *Momentum*, **8**, 3, pp. 10–19.

MEASOR, L. (1985) 'Critical incidents in the classroom: Identities, choices and careers', in BALL, S.J. and GOODSON, I.F. (eds) *Teachers Lives and Careers*, London: Falmer Press, pp. 61–78.

MECHIKOFF, R. and ESTES, S. (1993) *A History and Philosophy of Sport and Physical Education*, Madison, Wis.: Brown and Benchmark.

MILLER, S.C., BREDMEIER, B.J.L. and SHIELDS, D.L.L. (1997) 'Sociomoral education through physical education with at-risk children', *Quest*, 49, pp. 114–29.

MIRACLE, A.W., and REES, R.R. (1994) *Lessons of the Locker Room: The Myth of School Sports*, New York: Prometheus Books.

MOREIRA, H., SPARKES, A.C. and FOX, K. (1995) 'Physical education teachers and job commitment: A preliminary analysis', *European Physical Education Review*, **1**, 2, pp. 122–36.

MORGAN, R.E. (1974) *Concerns and Values in Physical Education*, London, G. Bell and Sons Ltd.

MYRLE JAMES, J. (1967) *Education and Physical Education*, London: G. Bell and Sons.

NIAS, J. (1981) 'Commitment and motivation in primary school teachers', *Educational Review*, 33, pp. 181–90.

NODDINGS, N. (1984) *Caring: A Feminine Approach to Ethics and Moral Education*, Berkeley: University of California Press.

OGLIVIE, B. and TUTKO, T. (1971) 'Sport: If you want to build character, try something else', *Psychology Today*, 5, pp. 60–3.

ORLICK, T. (1990) *In Pursuit of Excellence*, Champaign, Ill.: Human Kinetics.

O'SULLIVAN, M., SIEDENTOP, D. and TANNEHILL, D. (1994) 'Breaking out: Codependency of high school physical education', *Journal of Teaching in Physical Education*, 13, pp. 421–8.

PAUL, J. (1996) 'Centuries of change: Movement's many faces', *Quest*, **48**, 4, pp. 531–45.

PEARS, D. (1971) *What is Knowledge*? Wiltshire: George, Allen and Unwin.

PENNEY, D. and EVANS, J. (1997) 'Naming the game: Discourse domination in physical education and sport in England and Wales', *European Physical Education Review*, **3**, 1, pp. 21–32.

PENNEY, D. and HARRIS, J. (1997) 'Extra-curricular physical education: More of the same for the more able?', *Sport, Education and Society*, **2**, 1, pp. 41–54.

PETERS, R.S. (1966) *Ethics and Education*, London: Allen and Unwin.

PHENIX, P. (1964) *Realms of Meaning*, New York: McGraw Hill.

POWNEY, J. and WATTS, M. (1987) *Interviewing in Educational Research*, London: Routledge and Kegan Paul.

PRING, R. (1976) *Knowledge and Schooling*, London: Open Books.

REDDIFORD, G. (1983) 'The importance of physical activity', *Momentum*, **8**, 3, pp. 20–6.

REID, A. (1996a) 'The concept of physical education in current curriculum and assessment policy in Scotland', *European Physical Education Review*, **2**, 1, pp. 7–18.

REID, A. (1996b) 'Knowledge, practice and theory in physical education', *European Physical Education Review*, **2**, 2, pp. 94–104.

REID, A. (1997) 'Value pluralism and physical education', *European Physical Education Review*, **3**, 1, pp. 6–20.

ROG, J. (1986) 'Everyone seems satisfied', *Journal of Physical Education, Recreation and Dance*, **57**, 4, pp. 53–6.

ROVEGNO, I. and KIRK, D. (1995) 'Articulations and silences in socially critical work on physical education: Toward a broader agenda', *Quest*, 47, pp. 447–74.

RUNCIMAN, W.G. (1983) *A Treatise on Social Theory. Vol.1. The Methodology of Social Theory*, Cambridge: University Press.

RYLE, G. (1949) *The Concept of Mind*, London: Hutchinson.

SAGE, G. (1990) *Power and Ideology in American Sport: A Critical Perspective*, Champaign, Ill.: Human Kinetics.

SAGE, G. (1996) 'Reaction to the role of sport pedagogy', *Quest*, **48**, 4, pp. 451–2.

SCHEMPP, P.G. (1993) 'Constructing professional knowledge: A case study of an experienced high school teacher', *Journal of Teaching in Physical Education*, **13**, 1, pp. 2–23.

SHARP, N.C.C. (1994) Honorary Doctorate Citation to Mr J. Charlton, University of Limerick, Ireland, October 1994.

SHEILDS, D.L.L. and BREDEMEIER, B.J.L. (1995) *Character Development and Physical Activity*, Champaign, Ill.: Human Kinetics.

SIKES, P.J. (1988) 'Growing old gracefully? Age, identity and physical education', in EVANS, J. (ed.) *Teachers, Teaching and Control in Physical Education*, London: Falmer Press, pp. 21–40.

SIKES, P., MEASOR, L. and WOODS, P. (1985) *Teacher Careers: Crises and Continuities*, London: Falmer Press.

SIEDENTOP, D. (1987) 'The theory and practice of sport education', in BARETTE, G.T., FEINGOLD, R.S., ROGER REES, C. and PIERON, M. (eds) *Myths, Models and Methods in Sport Pedagogy*, Proceedings of the Adelphi-AIESEP 1985 World Sport Conference, August 19–22, Adelphi University, New York, Champaign, Il.: Human Kinetics Publishers, Inc.

SPARKES, A.C. (1987) 'Strategic rhetoric: A constraint in changing the practice of teachers', *British Journal of Sociology of Education*, 8, pp. 37–54.

SPARKES, A.C. (1989) 'Health related fitness: A case of innovation without change', *British Journal of Physical Education*, **20**, 2, pp. 60–2.

SPARKES, A.C. (1992) 'The paradigms debate: An extended review and a celebration of difference', in SPARKES, A. (ed.), *Research in Physical Education and Sport: Exploring Alternative Visions*, London: Falmer Press, pp. 9–60.

SPARKES, A.C. (1995) 'Writing people: Reflections on the dual crises of representation and legitimation in qualitative inquiry', *Quest*, 47, pp. 158–95.

SPARKES, A.C. and TEMPLIN, T.J. (1992) 'Life histories and physical education teachers: Exploring the meanings of marginality', in SPARKES, A.C. (ed.) *Research in Physical Education and Sport: Exploring Alternative Visions*, London: Falmer Press, pp. 118–45.

SPARKES, A.C., TEMPLIN, T. and SCHEMPP, P. G. (1990) 'The problematic nature of a career in a marginal subject: Some implications for teacher education programs', *Journal of Education for Teaching*, **16**, 1, pp. 3–28.

STAKE, R.E. (1995) *The Art of Case Study Research*, Thousand Oaks, Ca.: Sage.

STEVENSON, C.L. (1975) 'Socialization effect of participation in sport: A critical review of the research', *Research Quarterly*, 46, pp. 287–301.

STROOT, S. (1994) 'Contemporary crisis or emerging reform? A review of secondary physical education', *Journal of Teaching in Physical Education*, 13, pp. 333–41.

STROOT, S., COLLIER, C., O'SULLIVAN, M. and ENGLAND, K. (1994) 'Contextual hoops and hurdles: Workplace conditions in secondary physical education', *Journal of Teaching in Physical Education*, 13, pp. 342–60.

SUGRUE, C. (1997) *Complexities of Teaching: Child-centred Perspectives*, London: Falmer Press.

SUTTON-SMITH, B. (1973) 'Games: The socialization of conflict', *Canadian Journal of History and Physical Education*, **4**, 1, pp. 1–7.

TALBOT, M. (1996) 'Myths and mythologies — women and sport', Paper presented at Congreso Internationale de Education Fisica, Deporte Recreation Para La Mujer Insitituto Pedagogico Barquisimelo, Venezuela, October 28.

TALBOT, M. (1987) 'Physical education and school sport into the 1990s', The PEA Fellows Lecture, London, December.

TEMPLIN, T. (1989) 'Running on ice: A case study of the influence of work place conditions on a secondary school physical educator', in TEMPLIN, T. and SCHEMPP, P. (eds) *Socialization into Physical Education: Learning to Teach*, Indianapolis, IN.: Benchmark, pp. 165–95.

TEMPLIN, T., SPARKES, A., GRANT, B. and SCHEMPP, P. (1994) 'Matching the self: The paradoxical case and life history of a late career teacher/coach', *Journal of Teaching of Physical Education*, 13, pp. 274–94.

TEMPLIN, T., SPARKES, A.C. and SCHEMPP, P. (1991) 'The professional life cycle of a retired physical education teacher: A tale of bitter disengagement', *The Physical Education Review*, 14, pp. 143–56.

THORPE, R. (1996) 'Physical education: Beyond the curriculum', in ARMSTRONG, N. (ed.) *New Directions in Physical Education*, London: Cassell, pp. 144–56.

TINNING, R. (1991) 'Teacher education pedagogy: Dominant discourses and the process of problem setting', *Journal of Teaching in Physical Education*, 11, pp. 1–20.

TINNING, R., KIRK, D., EVANS, J. and GLOVER, S. (1994) 'School physical education: A crisis of meaning', *Changing Education*, **1**, 2, pp. 13–15.

VICKERS, J. (1992) 'While Rome burns — Meeting the challenge of the reform movement in education', *Journal of Physical Education, Recreation and Dance*, **63**, 7, pp. 80–7.

WHITE, J.P. (1973) *Towards a Compulsory Curriculum*, London: RKP.

WILLIAMS, J.F. (1964) *The Principles of Physical Education* (8th edition), Philadelphia: W.B. Saunders Co.

WOLCOTT, H. (1990) 'On seeing — and rejecting — validity in qualitative research', in EISNER, E. and PESHKIN, A. (eds) *Qualitative Inquiry in Education*, New York: Teachers' College Press, pp. 121–52.

WOLCOTT, H. (1994) *Transforming Qualitative Data*, London: Sage.

References

WOODS, P. (1990) *Teacher Skills and Strategies*, London: Falmer Press.

WOODS, P. (1980) *Teacher Strategies*, London: Croon Helm.

WOODS, P. (1979) *The Divided School*, London: Routledge and Kegan Paul.

WRIGHT MILLS, C. (1959) *The Sociological Imagination*, Harmondsworth: Penguin.

YEE, S. (1990) *Careers in the Classroom: When Teaching is More Than a Job*, New York: Teachers College Press.

Index

ability, mixed teaching, 30, 49–50
achievement, Laura's views, 51
administration, 27, 54, 130–1
Almond, L., 16
Appleyard, B., 113
Armour, K.M., 92, 108, 114, 125
Arnold, 22, 36–41, 128, 132
  administration, 131
  background, 124
  caring, 111, 112
  college, 39, 126
  commitment, 124
  examinations, 37, 100
  family, 38, 125
  health and fitness, 36, 97
  identity, 129, 130
  role models, 119
  side-bet, 128
  sport, 80, 86
  status, 38, 94
Arnold, P.J., 87–8, 116, 137–8
Atkinson, P., 7, 9

Ball, S., 131
Barton, L., 7
Beck, M., 84
Becker, H.S., 9, 35, 124, 128
Bell, L.A., 16, 17, 126
Bredemeier, B.J.L., 116, 117, 135
Brooker, R., 17, 101–2, 117
  caring, 111
  definitions, 83, 85
  health and fitness, 97
  status, 84, 104, 108
Buber, M., 111
Burgess, R.G., 124

Cale, L., 99
career progression, 17–18, 123–33, 135–6
caring, 17, 50–1, 53, 108–22
Carlisle, R., 96, 102
Carr, D., 90
Chelladurai, P., 79, 92
child-centred teaching, 49, 109, 112,
  113–14
Clapp, A.J., 99
clubs
  see also extra-curricular activities
  Arnold's views, 37
  Diane's views, 42
  Edgar's views, 56
  Enterprise High School, 47
  Jane's views, 23
  Maggie's views, 67
Cole, M., 129
college experience, 126–7
  see also case studies
Collier, C., 17
Colquhoun, D., 98
commitment, 42, 44, 48, 52, 123–4, 128
confidence, 55, 110, 116
Connell, R.W., 120
critical incidents, 124
Curtner-Smith, M.D., 99

Davies, B., 6, 84
Diane, 22, 42–6
  background, 125
  career, 129
  caring, 121
  college, 44, 126
  enthusiasm, 43, 128
  examinations, 43, 100

PE's purpose, 88
role models, 119
social development, 115
sport distinction, 42, 80–1
Dodds, P., 126
Doolittle, S., 126
Dowling Naess, F.J., 97, 103, 108, 125, 127, 129, 130
dualism, 24, 86–7, 115, 134

Edgar, 47, 54–9, 129
administration, 131
caring, 111–12
commitment, 124
enthusiasm, 54, 56
family background, 125–6
health and fitness, 97
PE's purpose, 88
social development, 114
sport distinction, 81
status, 94–5
Elbaz, F., 21
England, K., 17
enthusiasm, 128–9
Diane, 43, 128
Edgar, 54, 56
Grant, 128
Laura, 48–9, 51, 128
Maggie, 62, 66, 128, 129
Estes, S., 115
Evans, J., 6, 16, 101, 113, 117, 118
careers, 131–2
definitions, 83
health, 98
status, 84
examinations, 5–6, 26, 30–1, 100–2
Arnold's views, 37, 100
Diane's views, 43
GCSEs, 5–6, 24, 26, 31, 94, 100
extra-curricular programme
Edgar's views, 56, 58
Grant's views, 70, 73
Laura's views, 51, 52, 53
Maggie's views, 63, 66–7

family background, 125
see also case studies

Fernandez-Balboa, J.M., 90, 97, 137, 140
fitness, 63, 97–100, 135
Arnold's views, 36
Grant's views, 71, 72
Pete's views, 30
Fox, K., 17, 93, 103–4, 118

Geertz, C., 8, 10
gender
mixed teaching, 31–2, 49–50
single-sex teaching, 50, 56–7
George, L., 130
Giroux, H.A., 106, 107
Glover, S., 83
Grant, 14, 70–6
background, 125
caring, 109, 121, 122
college, 74–5, 126
commitment, 123–4
enthusiasm, 128
health and fitness, 71, 97
role models, 119
sport distinction, 72, 82
status, 76, 95
Grant, B., 123

Hammersley, M., 7, 9
Hargreaves, D.H., 139
Harris, J., 99, 140
Harrison, P., 16
health education, 30, 36, 97–100, 135
Grant's views, 71, 97
Jane's views, 24
Maggie's views, 63, 97–8
Hirst, P.H., 83, 88, 89, 113
Holt, R., 115

Jane, 21, 23–8, 127
administration, 27, 130–1
background, 124
caring, 110, 112, 121, 122
college, 26, 126
commitment, 124
enthusiasm, 128–9
examinations, 100
fitness, 97
PE's purpose, 88

pupil relationships, 120
sport distinction, 24, 80
status, 24, 94

Keddie, N., 86
Kegan, R., 110
Kerr, I.G., 99
Kirk, D., 17, 85, 110, 117, 130, 139,
    140–1
  cognitive skills, 90
  definitions, 83
  health education, 135
  research, 137
Kretchmar, S., 104–5, 140
Kuga, D.J., 79, 92

Laura, 14, 47, 48–53, 128
  administration, 130
  background, 125
  caring, 50–1, 53, 108, 110
  college, 51–2, 126, 127
  commitment, 123
  enthusiasm, 48–9, 51, 128
  examinations, 100
  PE's purpose, 88
  role models, 119, 125
  social development, 115
  sport distinction, 49, 81
  status, 94
Lawn, M., 7
Laws, C., 16
Lee, M., 116
Locke, L., 8, 106

Macdonald, D., 17, 101–2, 117
  caring, 111
  definitions, 83, 85
  health and fitness, 97
  status, 84, 104, 108
Maggie, 15, 62–9, 99
  caring, 110, 121, 122
  college, 66, 126, 127
  commitment, 123–4
  enthusiasm, 62, 66, 128, 129
  health, 63, 97–8
  National Curriculum, 86
  PE name change, 64–5, 83

role models, 118
social development, 115
sport distinction, 64, 81–2
status, 95
Major, J., 6
Mardle, G., 25
Maxwell, J.A., 8–9
Meakin, D.C., 85–6, 90
Measor, L., 123, 124
Mechikoff, R., 115
Metheney, E., 136
Miller, S.C., 135
Miracle, A.W., 116
moral development, 17, 108, 109, 113,
    114–18, 135
Moreira, H., 17, 93, 103–4, 118, 123,
    127–8, 130
Morgan, R.E., 93, 95, 96–7, 98, 117–18
Myrle James, J., 95–6, 99, 104, 106, 137

National Curriculum, 72, 85, 86
  health, 98, 99
  practical focus, 97
  sport distinction, 82, 84
Noddings, N., 17, 108–9, 110, 111–12,
    118, 119, 120

Oglivie, B., 116
Orlick, T., 116
O'Sullivan, M., 17, 100–1, 107, 108,
    120

Paul, J., 93, 98, 101, 102–3, 136, 138
Pears, D., 88
Penney, D., 6, 16, 84, 101, 113, 117–18,
    140
Pete, 22, 29–35, 96, 127, 128, 132
  caring, 109, 110, 112, 121, 122
  college, 33, 126
  commitment, 124
  examinations, 30–1, 100
  health and fitness, 30, 97
  identity, 129–30
  role models, 32–3, 119, 125
  sport distinction, 82
  status, 94
Peters, R.S., 17, 87, 88

Phenix, P., 88
Placek, J.H., 126
Powney, J., 7
Pring, R., 83, 85, 89, 92, 113, 114

Reddiford, G., 90
Rees, R.R., 116
Reid, A., 84, 88, 115, 138
  dualism, 86, 87
  PE's value, 96
  status, 84, 93
  theoretical knowledge, 90–1, 101
  well-being, 98
Rog, 123
role models, 32–3, 39, 109, 118–21,
  125
Rovegno, I., 17, 110, 117
Runciman, W.G., 8
Ryle, G., 24, 88–9

Sage, G., 79, 117
Schempp, P.G., 17, 93, 101, 103, 106,
  123, 131
sexism, 29, 32, 38
Sharp, N.C.C., 140
Sheilds, D.L.L., 116, 117, 135
side-bets, 35, 124, 128, 129
Siedentop, D., 83, 100–1, 107, 139
Sikes, P., 42, 123, 127, 128
social development, 17, 55, 108, 109,
  113, 114–18, 135
Sparkes, A.C., 9, 11, 17, 93, 98, 131,
  132
  career satisfaction, 123
  caring, 118
  reflexivity, 7, 8
  status, 103–4
  strategic rhetoric, 38, 122, 128
sport, 125–6
sport distinction, 3, 15–16, 79–92, 134,
  139–40
  Diane's views, 42, 80–1
  Grant's views, 72, 82
  Jane's views, 24, 80
  Laura's views, 49, 81
  Maggie's views, 64, 81–2
Sport, Raising the Game, 6, 15–16, 82

Stake, R.E., 8, 9
status, 3, 16–17, 18, 84–5, 93–107,
  134–6, 139
  Arnold's views, 38, 94
  career advancement, 132
  caring solution, 108
  Jane's views, 24, 94
  sport distinction, 87
Stevenson, C.L., 116
strategic rhetoric, 38, 121–2, 128
Stroot, S., 17, 97, 104, 125, 126
  definitions, 83
  social aims, 98
  status, 93
  support, 106–7
Sugrue, C., 113, 114, 119
Sutton-Smith, B., 116

Talbot, M., 15, 84, 117
Tannehill, D., 100–1, 107
teamwork, 110
  see also clubs
Templin, T., 8, 9, 93, 131, 132
  career satisfaction, 123
  reflexivity, 7
  role models, 125
  status, 17
Terkel, 7, 9
theoretical knowledge, 24, 32, 75, 90–1,
  100–1
Thorpe, R., 83–5
Tinning, R., 83, 85, 87, 96, 101
Tomlinson,-, 106
Tutko, T., 116

Vickers, J., 100

Walker, M., 25
Watts, M., 7
White, J.P., 17, 88
Williams, J.F., 95
Williams, T., 131–2
Wolcott, H., 7, 9, 11
Woods, P., 7, 25, 123, 127
Wright Mills, C., 6, 18

Yee, S., 123